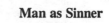

Man as Sinner

LAYMAN'S LIBRARY OF CHRISTIAN DOCTRINE

Man as Sinner

JOHN H. McCLANAHAN

BROADMAN PRESS
Nashville, Tennessee

Unless otherwise noted, Scripture quotations are from the Revised Standard Version of the Bible, copyrighted 1946, 1952, © 1971, 1973.

Scripture quotations marked (KJV) are from the King James Version of the Bible.

Scripture quotations marked (Phillips) are reprinted with permission of Macmillan Publishing Co., Inc. from J. B. Phillips: *The New Testament in Modern English,* Revised Edition. © J. B. Phillips 1958, 1960, 1972.

Library of Congress Cataloging in Publication Data

McClanahan, John H., 1929-
 Man as sinner.

 (Layman's library of Christian doctrine; v. 7)
 1. Sin. 2. Man (Christian theology) 3. Theology,
Doctrinal—Popular works. 4. Baptists—Doctrines.
I. Title. II. Series.
BT715.M37 1987   233   84-20036
ISBN 0-8054-1637-4

Foreword

The *Layman's Library of Christian Doctrine* in sixteen volumes covers the major doctrines of the Christian faith.

To meet the needs of the lay reader, the *Library* is written in a popular style. Headings are used in each volume to help the reader understand which part of the doctrine is being dealt with. Technical terms, if necessary to the discussion, will be clearly defined.

The need for this series is evident. Christians need to have a theology of their own, not one handed to them by someone else. The *Library* is written to help readers evaluate and form their own beliefs based on the Bible and on clear and persuasive statements of historic Christian positions. The aim of the series is to help laymen hammer out their own personal theology.

The books range in size from 140 pages to 168 pages. Each volume deals with a major part of Christian doctrine. Although some overlap is unavoidable, each volume will stand on its own. A set of the sixteen-volume series will give a person a complete look at the major doctrines of the Christian church.

Each volume is personalized by its author. The author will show the vitality of Christian doctrines and their meaning for everyday life. Strong and fresh illustrations will hold the interest of the reader. At times the personal faith of the authors will be seen in illustrations from their own Christian pilgrimage.

Not all laymen are aware they are theologians. Many may believe they know nothing of theology. However, every person believes something. This series helps the layman to understand what he believes and to be able to be "prepared to make a defense to anyone who calls him to account for the hope that is in him" (1 Pet. 3:15, RSV).

To
Rosalind, my wife
and
our children
David, Leanne, Rosalind, Stephen, Laura
and
our grandson
Matt

Preface

Do you remember Archie Bunker from his heyday in the television series, "All in the Family"? From his chair-throne in the living room of his very middle-class house in Queens, New York, Archie made grand pronouncements about many areas of American life. Drama critics said that he never completely filled the role of an updated Everyman for this era, but many of us did often see ourselves in his dogmatic lines.

Some of Archie's comments could well set the tone for this book on sin. For example, reflecting a smug sense of pride, Archie did not look upon himself as a sinner. "My religion is simple," Archie once said. "The Ten Commandments, that's my religion. I call 'em the 'Big Ten' *and I keep 'em too!*"[1]

Such unabashed self-righteousness often appeared in Archie's conversation with his wife Edith:

> EDITH: I was just thinking. In all the years we been married, you never once said you was sorry.
> ARCHIE: Edith, I'll gladly say that I'm sorry—*if I do anything wrong.*[2]

Bless Edith's heart for putting up with such a "Mr. Perfect" all those years!

Comments from other careful observers have not seen human nature to be so simplistically good. Pascal looked upon man as being an unfathomable puzzle: "What a chimera then is man! What a novelty! What a monster, what a chaos, what a contradiction, what a prodigy!"[3] Shakespeare marveled at the mystery of human nature: "What a piece of work is a man! How noble in reason! how infinite in faculty! in form, in moving how express and admirable! in action how like an angel! in apprehension how like a god! the beauty of the world! the paragon of animals! And yet, to me, what is *this quintessence of dust?*"[4]

T. S. Eliot saw men as "hollow" creatures. William Faulkner saw man in his earthiness—"the sum of his misfortunes . . . stalemate of dust and desire."⁵ Jean Paul Sartre spoke of man's life as being essentially a trappedness with "no exit." Eugene O'Neill despairingly saw man's glorious pilgrimage *in*gloriously stretching out and ending as "a long day's journey into night."

This volume will explore the darker side of human nature. In the pages which follow, you will quickly discover that sin is no laughing matter. To be sure, many contemporary people have tried to discard, or push away, the idea and relevance of sin in our modern age.

A distinguished American psychiatrist, Dr. Karl Menninger, pointed to the folly of this ploy, however, in his 1973 book entitled *Whatever Became of Sin?* This volume—likely the best-known American book on sin to be published in the past fifteen years—was not written by a professional theologian, but by a professional physician.

The concept of sin is far more than a mere complex or inhibition which we may psychologically outgrow. The idea of sin points to an area of personal, moral evil which is awesomely real in the world where each of us lives. This book proposes to present a serious examination of the idea of sin in down-to-earth terms which can easily be understood.

Although the word *man* appears in the title of this book, sin is not a uniquely masculine experience. Neither is sin a feminine phenomenon only. The essential "humanness" of sin includes all individuals. Menninger summarized his beliefs on the subject of sin in this statement:

> I believe there is "sin" which is expressed in ways which cannot be subsumed under verbal artifacts such as "crime," "disease," "delinquency," "deviancy." There is immorality; there is unethical behavior; there is wrongdoing. And . . . there is usefulness in retaining this concept, and indeed the word, SIN.⁶

Thus acknowledging the reality of our subject matter, I invite you to join me in a serious study of the Christian doctrine of human sin.

Notes

1. Spencer Marsh, *God, Man, and Archie Bunker* (New York: Harper and Row, 1975), p. 85.

2. Ibid., p. 30.

3. Blaise Pascal, *Pensees,* Sect. VII, No. 434.

4. William Shakespeare, *Hamlet,* II, ii, 315-24.

5. Quoted by William R. Mueller, *The Prophetic Voice of Modern Fiction* (New York: Association Press, 1959), p. 113.

6. Karl Menninger, *Whatever Became of Sin?* (New York: Hawthorn Books, Inc., p. 1973), p. 46.

Contents

1

What's Wrong with Us?

In a family of three, the only child neared school age. The little girl began to be very independent—even stubborn. She was often in open conflict with her parents. One afternoon, the little girl and her mother had a rather sharp disagreement over the little girl's failure to put up her toys and straighten the den area where she had been playing. Because of her sullen refusal to obey, her mother sent the young girl upstairs to her room. This enforced isolation was her punishment. The little girl was to remain in her room until her father came home from work later that afternoon.

The little girl reluctantly stomped up the stairs. As she walked down the hallway, she passed the open door to her parents' bedroom. It was also the place where her mother sewed. A lovely new party dress, which the mother had just finished, was lying across the bed. She was planning to wear the new dress to a party the next evening. The little girl dashed impetuously into the room and picked up the pinking shears from the sewing table and cut the dress into shreds. Tossing the mangled dress back on the bed, the girl put the scissors back on the sewing table. Then she ran to her own room.

After a while, the mother decided to check on her daughter. When passing her own bedroom door, she noticed that the party dress had been moved and rumpled. She walked quickly to the bedside and picked up the dress. Her careful work had been ruined. In a moment of frustrating despair, she threw herself across the bed and began to cry uncontrollably.

Down the hallway, the little girl heard her mother's sobs. Like the drawing power of a magnet, her mother's tears pulled the little girl out of her room and down the hall to the doorway where she could see her mother lying on the bed.

The little girl wanted to run to her mother and give her a big, comforting hug. But an invisible wall, like ice, seemed to freeze her in her place. Torn within by her childlike sense of love and guilt, the little girl herself began to cry. Inching forward toward her mother, she began to say ever so softly and plaintively, "Take me back, Mother! Please, Mother, take me back!"[1]

No single human story can ever be a full analogy of our human predicament. This incident, however, does come close. All of us are like that little girl. We have been born into a good and beautiful world, being given life by God the Creator. We all bear a remarkable resemblance to Him, not in physical appearance but in personal and spiritual traits. All of us were created by God "in his own image" (Gen. 1:27). The psalmist wrote, "It is he that made us, and we are his; we are his people, and the sheep of his pasture" (Ps. 100:3).

God has given us guidelines on how to live. He gives us responsibilities, and He calls for our obedience. But, like the little girl, we are not always willing to obey. We are stubbornly independent; we cut, tear, and destroy the beautiful way of life which God wants us to enjoy. Often we hurt the people who are nearest us. As we cut ourselves off from our own kind, we also shut ourselves off from God.

If we listen carefully, we may hear God crying. The sobs of God remind us of both our distance from Him and our desire to return to Him. For when we are estranged from God, we have cut ourselves off from the ground of our own being (Acts 17:28). The Bible teaches us that this is basically what is wrong with all of us.

Where Are You?

The question, "Where are you?" may appear quite superficial. It calls to mind the old nonsense story of a traveling salesman who lost his way and asked a farm boy for directions. To each of the salesman's questions—Do you know how far it is to the next town? Do you know where this road goes? Do you know how to get to the main highway?—

the boy replied with an apologetic no. In disgust the salesman retorted: "Son, you don't know very much, do you?" The boy responded: "Well, sir, I'm not lost!"

In the context of my illustration, the question, "Where are you?" has a geographical frame of reference. Being lost has to do with being uncertain as to specific location. Lostness in this sense is a matter of location on a map. Most of us would answer this question something like this: "Well, at least I know where I am! I am in my hometown, in my home state, in my country, on the North American continent, on the planet earth, in the solar system. Yes sir, I do know where I am!"

When asked in the context of biblical faith, however, "Where are you?" is not primarily a question concerned with geographical location. As a religious question, it is more profound and penetrating. It probes our basic relationships in life: Where are you in relation to yourself? in relation to other people? in relation to God? The perceptive Dutch theologian, Hendrik Kraemer, thought this question was one of the most challenging summons in the Bible.[2]

When understood theologically, the question underscores God's initiative in discovering man where he is and restoring broken communication or relationship with Him.

This question is basic to the revealed faith of the Bible. It is central in Genesis 1—11. These eleven chapters are like a theological introduction to the Old Testament. They state beautifully Israel's creation faith. "In the beginning God created the heavens and the earth" (Gen. 1:1). All of God's creation was good. The Genesis account declares repeatedly that what God made was good (vv. 4,12,18,21,25).

No sign of Greek dualism between matter and spirit, body and soul, is found in the Hebrew account of creation. Quite pointedly, Genesis affirms that the creation of humankind as male and female was good. We should note that our sexuality was not just *plain* good; it was "*very* good" (v. 31, author's italics).

Man is a part of the created order. He shares similarities with the rest of the natural world. Yet man is dissimilar from the rest of creation because he is the crowning glory of God's creative activity. Man is, indeed, dust and divinity. The language of Genesis beautifully expresses this mystery: "Then the Lord God formed man of dust from the ground, and breathed into his nostrils the breath of life; and man became a living being" (Gen. 2:7). Man was given dominion and power over the rest of creation (Gen. 1:28). He was created in the image of God (v. 27), that is, he was created to have communion and to live in loving relationship with God.

Although subject to the limitations of the created order, man existed with a unique kind of freedom. He was not God's automaton. Neither was man a puppet, or marionette, playacting upon the stage of history. Man was given the capacity to choose between good and evil. In the act of choosing, man asserted his freedom. Man's decision to disobey God violated his own nature. His evil choice was his inescapable sin. Because of his sin, man was estranged and isolated from God and his neighbor. In fact, when man broke community and relationship with God and his neighbor, he was actually breaking relationship within himself and bringing destruction upon himself. What was true for man in Eden is still true for man today.

Four incidents in the Genesis prologue describe the destructive effect of man's sin upon his essential relationships. The Garden of Eden incident points to the fact that sin disrupts man's harmonious relationship with himself and with God. Adam and Eve became ashamed and attempted to hide from God (Gen. 3:8). The murder of Abel by Cain shows that sin resulted in man's violating the image of God in his brother. Man's relationship with his fellowman was fragmented.

In the days of Noah, men forgot that they had any relationship with God. They exalted the dirt of human nature. Each lived as though he was an animal—d-o-g, if you please. In the drama at the Tower of Babel, men forgot their terrestrial mooring. Each became guilty of the ultimate revolt—trying to live as though he were a g-o-d. The destruction of the tower points to the brokenness which marks man's relationship with God.

Where are we? The opening chapters of the Bible declare that all people are alone and lost. What was history in Eden is actual life for us today. Man's original situation in the past is our situation today.

In the Genesis account, God appeared and asked man this thunderous question: "Adam, where art thou?" (Gen. 3:9, KJV). This is an inescapable question for all persons. As such, it points up the radical difference between the Greek and the Hebrew approaches to religion, to the nature of God and man.

The parallel Greek question or exhortation is "Know thyself!" The Greek philosophers believed that man can know himself in isolation by means of rational analysis and psychological probing. In this tradition, man addresses the summons to himself and considers that he is capable of doing what it says. God is viewed as being an aloof, distant deity, or unmoved mover, who is not directly concerned with the life of man.

In contrast to this, the Hebrew question, "Where are you?" implies a relationship in which there is some doubt as to man's exact location. Man does not address himself. He is addressed by God, who enters the plane of human existence and makes Himself known to man. In light of the total Genesis message, the implication of this question is that man will know himself only as he is discovered by God, and, as a consequence of this discovery, finds himself in adequate relationship with his neighbor and himself.

To distinguish three dimensions in man's basic relatedness—his relationship with God, his brother, and himself—is not to imply that the old Greek dualism is replaced by an Hebraic three-way division of man. First, last, and always, the Hebrews thought of man as being a totality, a body-soul unity. Rather than being separate compartments in man's nature, these three divisions of relationship blend into each other as the colors in the spectrum. The variations are there, but each so affects the other that they must be considered as a whole. Let us examine more closely these three relationships as they are presented in the four major incidents in the Genesis prologue.

The Error of Eden

The Garden of Eden incident deals poignantly with this dimension of man's existence: man's relationship with himself. Because of his disobedience and rebellious choice, man was estranged from himself. Man failed himself when he refused to pursue God's will; as a result, he was ashamed. Both Adam and Eve tried to cover themselves with crude clothing. Note the language of Genesis at this point: "Then the eyes of both were opened, and they knew that they were naked; and they sewed fig leaves together and made themselves aprons" (Gen. 3:7).

The idyllic joy of life in Eden was wiped out when the painful awareness of man's guilt invaded the depths of his consciousness. The Genesis narrative continues: "And they heard the sound of the Lord God walking in the garden in the cool of the day, and the man and his wife hid themselves from the presence of the Lord God among the trees of the garden. But the Lord God called to the man, and said to him, 'Where are you?' And he said, 'I heard the sound of thee in the garden, and I was afraid, because I was naked; and I hid myself'" (vv. 8-10).

In violating God's command, man violated the law of his own being. He was sent into exile "east of . . . Eden" (v. 24). Man was uprooted from his initial mooring and sent forth to live as a refugee upon the face of the earth. With penetrating truth, Genesis declares that man lost something in this experience which could never be regained: "He [God] drove out the man; and at the east of the garden of Eden he placed the cherubim, and a flaming sword which turned every way, to guard the way to the tree of life" (v. 24).

In this way, the Genesis narrative declares that something in the idyllic paradise of Eden was lost which would never be fully regained on earth. This, however, was only the beginning of man's problem.

The First Cain Mutiny

The story of Cain and Abel shows that man's evil choice affected his relationship with other people. When he destroyed his own inner peace, man also broke his sense of community with his brother. When he became false to himself, he became false to other people. Cain's denial that he was his brother's keeper (Gen. 4:9) is an expression of the brokenness which afflicts all human relationships.

Cain and Abel were sons of Adam and Eve (vv. 1-2). Cain was the firstborn son and, thus, the older brother. As brothers, Cain and Abel shared the same home, but they were not identical in their interests and gifts. As they grew toward maturity, their differences in temperament became more distinct. Like Adam, Cain was a gardener, or a row crop farmer—"a tiller of the ground" (v. 2). In contrast, Abel, the younger brother, was a herdsman—"a keeper of sheep" (v. 2). Throughout history, people from these two basic life-styles have been rivals. They have shared varying degrees of enmity toward one another.

In the course of time, probably as young adults, Cain and Abel reached the age of maturity when they wanted to present their own personal offerings unto God. They were no longer content for their parents to do that for them. They were both moving toward more mature levels of religious understanding and responsibility. This was all voluntary on their part. Genesis does not indicate that either God or their parents requested this of them.

Each brother brought something representative of his own industry and hard work. Cain brought a produce offering—"the fruit of the ground" (v. 3). Abel brought animals from his herd—"the firstlings of his flock" (v. 4). Genesis reports this response from the Lord to these two different offerings: "The Lord had regard for Abel and his offering, but for Cain and his offering he had no regard" (vv. 4-5). Abel's offering was acceptable to God, but Cain's offering was not acceptable.

What was the difference between the two gifts at the altar? Why did God accept what Abel brought and not accept what Cain brought? It seems unlikely that God's response was due to the actual material offering which the two brothers brought. God did not primarily accept Abel's offering because it had blood in it and refuse Cain's offering because it was bloodless. We know from the later history of Israel that the produce offering, or "cereal offering" (Lev. 2:1), became a principle offering in the Jewish sacrificial system. Clyde T. Francisco's comment is to the point in this regard: "Obviously God was more pleased with the blood offering, which was the primary one in the Old Testament, but he would not have rejected the produce except as a sin offering. There is no indication here that a sin offering is the issue."[3]

The Genesis account does say that Abel brought the "firstlings of his flock and of their fat portions" (Gen. 4:4). In other words, Abel brought the very best that he had. But in contrast, Cain brought only "the fruit of the ground" (v. 3). It is a noticeable absence that Genesis does not mention any "*first*fruits" at this point. But an argument from silence does not build a strong case.

More likely the key point of difference between the two offerings is not the material the brothers brought in their hands, but rather the attitude they held in their hearts. As Jesus said later, "So if you are offering your gift at the altar, and there remember that your brother has something against you, leave your gift there before the altar and go; first be reconciled to your brother, and then come and offer your gift" (Matt. 5:23). Jesus said a gift of worship and adoration to God is not acceptable from a heart which harbors jealousy and hatred toward a fellow human being. Thus is was not what Cain and Abel brought to God in their hands. It was not an issue of carrots versus cows or sweet potatoes versus sheep or plant cells versus animal tissue. It was a matter of the heart.

Cain was "very angry" (Gen. 4:5). His face fell. The Lord asked Cain: "Why are you angry? . . . If you do well, will you not be accepted? And if you do not do well, sin is couching at the door; its desire is for you, but you must master it" (vv. 6-7). The words suggest that the cause of Cain's dissatisfaction lay within himself. The phrase describing sin as "couching at the door" is quite graphic. It brings to mind the picture of a member of the cat family poised like steel, fixing to spring upon its prey.

The venom in Cain's heart spilled out into bloodshed. Cain picked a time when he and Abel were alone. Cain "rose up against his brother Abel, and killed him" (v. 8). The first murder was fratricide—a brother killing a brother. In many respects, all murder is such killing—a kinsman taking the life of another kinsman.

In this first murder, we can see just the corner of a much larger quilt— the whole long story of man's inhumanity to man—from Eden to Auschwitz. The peace of the human community—indeed, the peace of the human family—was shattered. Like breaking the placid surface of a pond by throwing in a stone, concentric circles from Cain's murder of Abel have moved out to touch every shore. This story is also about life today. We stand on the brink of being able to unleash nuclear holocaust. We may not only destroy our brothers, but also ourselves, if this kind of awesome power should be unsheathed.

As Adam and Eve had discovered, so Cain learned that sin has its demanding price. Denying that he bore any responsibility for his brother's well-being (v. 9), Cain also was sent out as an exile. He was to become "a fugitive and a wanderer on the earth" (v. 12), condemned to live in the land of Nod, east of Eden (v. 16). The implication is that Cain's sin of destroying his brother made it difficult for him to know enduring and meaningful human relationships of any kind.

The was-ness of Genesis again is the is-ness of our lives. It is not necessary to throw the stone, thrust the knife, fire the gun, or drop the bomb, in order to kill and destroy. With a piercing and disturbing insight, the Irish poet, Oscar Wilde, reminds us how easily anyone can ooze into the role of a killer:

> Yet each man kills the thing he loves,
> By each let this be heard,
> Some do it with a bitter look,
> Some with a flattering word,
> The coward does it with a kiss,
> The brave man with a sword![4]

Thus the peace of the human family was and is broken, yet the gravity of man's problem is even more severe than this.

The Moral Chaos of Noah's Day

In one sense, the problem of Adam and Eve in Eden centered around a kind of naive deceit and rebellion between God and one married couple. The tension with Cain and Abel focused on a single festering sibling rivalry which boiled over into outright anger and one murder. In the days of Noah, however, man's bent toward evil broke forth with the unrestrained force of a raging forest fire, which engulfed a whole civilization.

The Genesis account describes the moral chaos in this way: "The Lord saw the wickedness of man was great in the earth, and that every imagination of the thoughts of his heart was only evil continually" (6:5). We have noted that the Genesis language of creation makes man a remarkable composite of dust and divinity. In the days of Noah, men exalted the "dust"—or dirt—of their natures.

The people forgot that they had any kinship with God. They followed corrupt life-styles of overt wickedness, allowing their human existence to degenerate to an animal level. The people lived and loved as though they were dogs. The stench of such a culture rose to heaven as an offense to God. Genesis declares: "Now the earth was corrupt in God's sight, and the earth was filled with violence. And God saw the earth, and behold, it was corrupt; and all flesh had corrupted their way upon the earth" (vv. 11-12).

Clyde Francisco described these verses from Genesis as "the strongest statement concerning human depravity in the Old Testament."[5] Look how far man had fallen. From the level in God's early dawn of creation when everything was "very good" (1:31), man had fallen to the point that "every imagination . . . of his heart was only evil continually" (6:5).

Because of the moral mess which man had made, God was greatly disappointed. Genesis declares that "the Lord was sorry that he had made man on the earth, and it grieved him to his heart" (v. 6). God decided to destroy the earth. He spoke to Noah, "I have determined to make an end of all flesh; for the earth is filled with violence through them; behold, I will destroy them with the earth" (v. 13).

God instructed Noah to build an ark for the purpose of saving himself and his family, plus some of the animal life of the earth. Every other person and thing was to be destroyed. God said, "For behold, I will bring a flood of waters upon the earth, to destroy all flesh in which is the breath of life from under heaven; everything that is on the earth shall die" (v. 17). By forgetting any kinship they held with God, and by allowing life to drop to the lowest possible moral level, the people of Noah's day brought ruin upon themselves.

Helmut Thielicke, the well-known Evangelical pastor-preacher from Hamburg, Germany, wrote that the Genesis account of the Flood is far more than a lesson in ancient history.

> The powers of destruction are still present in the midst of creation. The atoms—did not God create them?—need only to be split, the bacteria let loose, hereditary factors monkeyed with, genes tampered with, and poisons need only to be distilled from the gifts of creation—oh yes, the powers of destruction are still with us and the heavenly ocean is still heaving and surging behind its dams. We live solely by the grace of God, who has fixed the bounds of destruction. . . . The dreadful secret of the world revealed in the first chapters of this old Book is that man is capable of *renouncing* and cutting himself off from this very grace which holds in check the power of destruction.[6]

Any one of us, or all of us together, can play too fast and too loose with what Thielicke called "that grace which guards the dikes of ruin."

But in his personal catalog for potential evil, man has the option of yet a graver sin. This brings us to the fourth key incident in the Genesis prologue.

The Rank Rebellion at Babel

The Genesis narrative tells us that, as men moved about on the face of the earth, they settled on a fertile plain in the land of Shinar (11:2). This is likely a general reference to the Mesopotamian Valley between the Tigris and the Euphrates Rivers. This was the central location of the old Babylonian Empire.

In a typical Babylonian city, the dominant building was the temple. In fact, cities tended to grow up around these sanctuaries, rather than the place of worship arising within the city. The dominant feature of a Babylonian temple was the tower, or the "ziggurat." The pyramid-shaped ziggurat was built in terrace fashion, each level being smaller than the previous level. In an urban center where all other buildings were only one story tall, the ziggurat was quite imposing. The top of a ziggurat was crowned with a small shrine, which was thought to be the abode of the gods. What Mount Olympus was to the Greeks, the ziggurat was to the Babylonians. The Genesis account of the Tower of Babel may reflect to some extent an influence from Babylonian architecture and thought.

The Genesis narrative reports that men came together to build a city and a tower: "Come, let us build ourselves a city, and a tower with its top in the heavens, and let us make a name for ourselves, lest we be scattered abroad upon the face of the whole earth" (v. 4).

God, however, was not pleased with this human endeavor. He came down and confused the language of the craftsmen so they could not complete their work (vv. 7-8). The unfinished city and the ruined tower together were called "Babel" (v. 9). The name itself is an interesting play on words. The Babylonian word meant "gate of God," but the Hebrew word referred to "confusion."

The building at Babel points to the root of man's problem. God created man for Himself. In God, man lives and moves and has his being. Man can realize his full potential only when he finds himself in loving, obedient relationship to God. The Babel incident, however, points to the fact that man is not content to be mere man. In his cleverness, he would build a tower that would reach up into the heavens. He would "make a name" (v. 4) for himself, apart from God's will and purpose. Indeed, man would build a tower which would pierce the blue dome of the sky. Climbing to the top of such a structure, man could usurp the place of God!

For man the creature to deny his basic finitude and aspire to be God is the rankest rebellion. Such action brings God's judgment. The tower was destroyed, and man was cut off from God, the sole ground of his being. Becoming further alienated from God also causes man to be further isolated from his fellow human beings. Communication became broken and difficult because men no longer spoke the same language.

In light of all this, we may conclude that the Genesis prologue declares straightforwardly that, left to himself, man is broken, alienated, divided, morally bankrupt, and confused. In the most profound sense, left to himself, man is utterly and completely *lost!*

Man is in trouble with his own self-image—embarrassed and ashamed because of his impetuous, disobedient behavior. Rather than living in loving relationship with his fellow human beings, man too easily comes to resent his brother. He is jealous and angry with his own peers. This inner attitude often spills over into violence and bloodshed.

Created to walk the narrow, knife's-edge role of being a creature made from dust, yet having the likeness of God, man is continually veering into the moral trap of trying either to play God or to live like a dog. Either extreme destroys the nature of man's being, because he is neither a god nor a dog. Man is a human.

The Genesis prologue declares that man's predicament is serious. His problem is not some slight surface injury which needs only the care of an adhesive strip. Man's problem—his sin—strikes at the very core of his personhood. Because of his sin, man stands in need not of cosmetic surgery but of heart surgery. Man needs to become a new creature.

The message of the Genesis prologue is not that man finally comes to himself. Left to himself, man only sinks deeper into the mire of his own sin. The biblical insight is that God comes to man. In search for man, God came calling, "Adam, where are you?" . . . "Cain, where is your brother?"

After the destruction of the Flood and the loss of a whole civilization, God started over again in His call to Noah. In the wake of the destruction of Babel and the confusion of language, God called Abraham (Gen. 12:1) to begin a new nation through which He would ultimately bless the entire world.

Before pursuing further these hints of reconciliation and salvation, let us examine some New Testament comments on the predicament of man.

Three Parables on Man's Plight

Luke reported that the publicans—or tax collectors—and sinners "were all drawing near to hear him [Jesus]" (15:1). The legalistic scribes and Pharisees resented the growing popularity which Jesus was enjoying with the people of the land. Their opposition to Jesus was beginning to solidify. They "murmured" against Jesus, spitefully saying, "This man receives sinners and eats with them" (v. 2).

By Jewish ritual law, publicans and sinners were unclean. From the Pharisees's point of view, Jesus defiled Himself by associating with such people. Can't you almost hear the malice in their voices, as they said, "He even *eats* with them"?

To set forth a basic commitment of His ministry, Jesus told these three parables about a lost sheep, a lost coin, and a lost son. These are Jesus' best-known parables. They deal directly with the predicament of man. Each parable stands on its own. But they have a common thread that ties them together: Something or someone is lost (Luke 15).

Becoming Lost by Accident

Jesus told of a shepherd who was caring for a hundred sheep as they grazed in the "wilderness" (vv. 3-7). One hundred sheep is a rather large flock for one shepherd to be tending. It is quite easy to see how one animal could have been lost from the shepherd's view. The shepherd did not realize his loss until the flock entered the sheepfold at the close of the grazing day. The shepherd counted the sheep as they passed under the shepherd's rod at the single door of the sheepfold. When the loss was discovered, the shepherd immediately secured the ninety-nine and sought the one lost sheep. The search, no doubt, was long and hard.

Someone asked a Palestinian shepherd, "How do sheep get lost?" The shepherd thought momentarily and then gave this reply, "They *nibble* themselves lost!" He explained that as sheep graze they may wander away from the flock. They may become distracted and forget to keep the shepherd in sight. They may focus their eyes on the ground, moving from one tuft of grass to the next, oblivious to the fact that the flock is going in a different direction. The sheep may fail to notice when the pastoral melody of the sheep bells is no longer heard.

Thus carelessly, unwittingly, largely oblivious to what they are doing, sheep may nibble themselves lost. To this reply, the person who asked the question said simply, "How like people!"

That kind of behavior is duplicated in the human family. Having been a pastor for almost thirty years, I have known of people in all kinds of personal trouble and difficulty. I have never known of anyone who said forthrightly, "Go away now, I'm going to make a mess of my life!" But I have seen countless people who really did mess up their lives. I have discovered that so often my friends "nibbled" themselves into sin. Inch by inch, bit by bit, they oozed into the quagmire of sin. Often they did not realize the direction of their lives until they had already arrived at its destination.

Becoming Lost at Home

In the second parable in this trilogy, Jesus told about something that was lost in a house (vv. 8-10). A certain woman who had ten silver coins discovered that one of them was missing. The coins might have been part of the woman's dowry, fastened to a headpiece which she wore on special occasions. As such, losing one of the coins would be comparable today to a young woman's losing a valued stone from her engagement ring. The missing coin might have been a part of a secret fund which this mother was saving to buy something special for another member of her family. Mothers in another era have called this kind of ready cash "egg money," or the "fruit jar fund." For families who lived near the edge of want all the time, the loss of one such coin would be devastating. Jesus might have been recalling a scene from His own childhood, when He saw His own mother search for a lost coin.

Whatever the exact circumstance, the woman's search was intense, perhaps even frantic. As Jesus told the story, He mentioned that the woman took a lighted lamp and searched "diligently" to find the lost coin (v. 8). When her search was successful, she called together her neighbors and friends to rejoice with her, "for I have found the coin which I had lost" (v. 9).

Lost at home has a haunting ring about it. Home, of all places, should be that area of life where all things are safe and secure. In the fourth quarter of the twentieth century, however, the phrase "Home, Sweet Home!" does not best describe our culture. Some observers have written that before the end of this century, we will see not a death *in* the family but a death *of* the family. Such dour predictions are unlikely extremes, but it is true that much of America's home front is crumbling. Divorce, child abuse, teenage suicide, and other home-related ills have reached epidemic stages in our society.

In the past fifty years, social scientists, working in the area of home and family relations, have amassed convincing evidence of the importance of an individual's early childhood in the formation of personality and character. What is done, said, and felt in the early years is often transcribed with indelible ink. Some of us are so scarred by experiences which came to us at home that we will spend the rest of our lives trying to understand our background and cope with our feelings. The "fruit" of life is to a great extent dependent on the "roots" of life. Most of us get our rootage, our foundation for character and belief, in the homes where we were nurtured.

A cross-stitch picture-saying, which my family treasures very much, hangs on a wall in our home. The needlework was done by our older daughter during her first year out of college in "the real world." She gave her mother and me the framed picture as a Christmas gift that year. It reads: "There are two lasting gifts we can give to our children—one is roots, the other wings!"

But what happens to the child who finds neither of these basic ingredients for life at home? The acid soil of homelife can cause tiny roots to wither and die. Life in such homes can result in low self-esteem so that wings are never realized and developed. No family is exempt from this possibility. The preacher's kids—or the children of any other busy person—may become victims of "child neglect" because their parents are always too involved doing God's work in the church and community to spend quality time with them. Even in affluent homes, where money is no problem, children can become "*poor,* little rich kids," impoverished by their lack of parental love and presence.

Original sin engulfs us all. But the person who is lost at home carries an even greater load of sin—a psychological load that at times seems heavier than any person could bear. How does a child who has never been loved at home come to believe that God is love? How does a child who has been abused or exploited at home ever learn to trust anyone, including God? Unfortunately, lost at home is often the epithet of many people in this generation.

Becoming Lost in a Far Country

The third parable in this trilogy is one of Jesus' best-known stories (vv. 11-32). The narrative unfolds around the lives of the two sons of a certain man, who must have been a rather wealthy landowner. In studying the parable, focus is usually placed on the younger son. Most of us know this as the parable of the prodigal son.

The younger son asked his father for his share of the family property (v. 12). The father evidently readily divided his property between his sons, with little question about the younger son's request. This was not initially a bad request from the younger son. By the Jewish law concerning the firstborn, the major part of the father's inheritance would have gone to the elder brother. Had the younger son remained at home on the farm, he likely would have become little more than an employee of his brother. It may well have been with genuine ambition and aspiration that the younger son requested his share of the inheritance. He may have wanted to see if he could make it on his own.

The younger son converted his inheritance into some kind of cash money, and "took his journey into a far country" (v. 13). The far country would have been outside Palestine, thus in Gentile territory. The great British statesman, Winston Churchill, wrote a little-known novel entitled *A Far Country.* Although it does not have to be, Churchill depicted the far country as an alien land where standards and ideals are quickly lost.

To this point in the parable, the younger son has done nothing more than create an opportunity whereby he might go off to seek his fortune. Young people in every generation, in one way or another, leave their communities to seek their fortunes. They go off to college or off to military service. They move to a larger city in search of better job opportunities. High school and college graduates scatter in a thousand ways. Such behavior is a sign of good initiative and purpose.

A popular song from the forties included this line, ". . . those far away places with their strange sounding names." The sentiment of that song is not as true today as when it was first written. The jet age has almost annihilated distance, at least as distance was once understood. For example, when my father was a child, a trip from the family farm into town by wagon and team—a distance of eight miles—took all day! Today, a businessman can leave New York City in the morning on the French *Concorde,* transact business in Paris, and return to New York that same evening—a distance of several thousand miles! The world has become a global village.

In terms of distance, there are no far away places as they were once understood. The story of the far country is no longer told in terms of miles. Today motives and mores, culture and customs, define the far country. The far country is still where things are different from home— in terms of food, lodging, people, responsibility, opportunity, ideas, loyalities, demands.

Being in a far country, however, does bring a new burst of freedom. Everything looks and sounds new and exciting. With money in his pockets, the younger son in Jesus' parable quickly made new friends. Rather quickly it became evident, however, that he was not mature enough to handle his freedom nor manage his money. Jesus reported that, too soon, the young man "squandered his property in loose living" (v. 13).

The road down tends to move in the fast lane. Building a successful life often seems to move at a snail's pace. The path of decline, however, tends to drop with the dizzy speed of a roller coaster. When the young man had spent his last dime, his luck took another turn for the worst. The far country where he was began to experience a famine. He was out of work. He was hungry. He began to know something which likely he had never known before. He was in want!

Had there been bread lines, soup kitchens, or rescue missions in that day, these would have been his daily fare. He finally found a job with a citizen in that country, working as a swineherder (v. 15). The depth of his need is illustrated by the fact that he slipped food for himself from the pods of the carob tree which he fed to the hogs. In disgust, he must have asked himself, "What's a nice Jewish boy like me doing in a place like this?"

The far country can become very real and contemporary when you spend a weekend on some university campuses or ride with the police vice squad in a large city near a military base. A few years ago, while preaching in revival services in an Eastern seaboard state, I was staying alone in a local motel. A national business seminar was also being held in the city. One night I was awakened by a conversation coming from an adjacent room. Through the thin walls of that motel, I could overhear the sad, shallow, shameful conversation of an out-of-town businessman entertaining a prostitute for the night. People still can get lost when they get away from home, and they can still squander much of their character and their substance in loose living.

Don Harbuck, one of my longtime pastor friends, told of a Sunday morning conversation which he had with his daughter years ago. The family was dressing for Sunday services. The little girl, who was about five years old at the time, asked her father, "Daddy, what are you going to preach about this morning?"

My friend replied by asking his daughter a question. Calling her by name, he said, "What would you like for me to preach about this morning?" The little girl thought for a moment, and then replied, "Tell a story about Jesus, and put me in it!"

This is just what these three parables are—stories about Jesus from Jesus; and we, all of us, are in them. They are parables including all persons. Too easily, any one of us can "nibble" himself lost. Even the best parents make some mistakes, leaving scars on their children. And sooner or later, all of us will be tempted to enter the fast lane which can lead to the far country with its heady, beckoning freedom—which actually is no freedom at all.

Paul's Painful Search for Self-Identity

In unforgettable parables, Jesus described sin with graphic images. He Himself, however, was without sin (Heb. 4:15; 1 Pet. 1:19). On the other hand, the man who wrote more letters in our New Testament than any other single person—Paul, the apostle—knew well the reality and deadly sting of sin. Paul's conversion to faith in Christ brought such a radical change in his life that his name was changed. Saul of Tarsus—the strict Pharisee, became Paul of Antioch—the first missionary apostle to the Gentiles.

As a Jew, Paul knew firsthand what it was to be "imprisoned under the power of the Law" (Gal. 3:23, Phillips). Before he became a Christian believer, Paul saw the Gentiles being utterly depraved—"separated from Christ, alienated from the commonwealth of Israel, and strangers to the covenants of promise, having no hope and without God in the world" (Eph. 2:12).

Paul wrote with conviction to the Romans, "All have sinned and fall short of the glory of God" (3:23). He was equally convinced that all people were "slaves of sin" (6:20) and that "the wages of sin is death" (v. 23).

Perhaps Paul's most vivid statement of the unrelenting grip of sin on his life, however, is found in his Letter to the Romans. Paul's description of his inner self comes close home to many of us.

> My own behaviour baffles me. For I find myself doing what I really loathe but not doing what I really want to do. Yet surely if I do things that I really don't want to do, I am admitting that I really agree that the Law is good. But it cannot be said that "I" am doing them at all—it must be sin that has made its home in my nature. And, indeed, I know from experience that the carnal side of my being can scarcely be called the home of good! I often find that I have the will to do good, but not the power. That is, I don't accomplish the good I set out to do, and the evil I don't really want to do I find I am always doing. Yet if I do things that I don't really want to do then it is not, I repeat, "I" who do them, but the sin which has made its home within me. My experience of the Law is that when I want to

do good, only evil is within my reach. My conscious mind wholeheart-
edly endorses the Law, yet I observe an entirely different principle at work
in my nature. This is in continual conflict with my conscious attitude, and
makes me an unwilling prisoner to the law of sin and death. In my mind I
am God's willing servant, but in my own nature I am bound fast, as I
say, to the law of sin and death. It is an agonizing situation, and who on
earth can set me free from the clutches of my own sinful nature?" (Rom.
7:15-24, J. B. Phillips).

A few years ago, I read this personal statement from Paul, as translated by J. B. Phillips, in a Sunday morning worship service. Several
people who were present that day made interesting comments about the
service. One man said, "I didn't know there was anything in the Bible
like those verses which you read this morning! I feel that way about
myself most of the time. I had no idea that Paul could have felt that way
about himself."

Later that week, an adult woman told me of her conversation with a
friend, who was also a church member. She told her friend, "I'm so glad
that you finally talked with the pastor about your problem!"

The friend replied, "But I haven't talked with him!"

A bit surprised, the first woman said, "Well, I just knew you had from
the Scripture and sermon which we heard at church last Sunday. It
seemed to fit your situation exactly!"

Her friend added, "It did just that. I had no idea that anyone in the
Bible would feel the same kind of inner conflict which I have known!"

Paul understood correctly that there was something wrong with him.
He defined that something in terms of the three letter word, *s-i-n*. In
phrases with which many of us can identify, Paul described his desperate
sense of being trapped in sin, and he cried out for deliverance. He concluded this stirring autobiographical passage with a statement of hope:
"I thank God there is a way out through Jesus Christ our Lord" (v. 25,
Phillips).

Thus We Conclude

What's wrong with us? The wisdom of the Bible reveals that, left to
ourselves, we are utterly lost. We are self-centered, grasping creatures

who are unwilling to follow even the minimal guidelines for life set forth by our Creator. We are jealous, spiteful persons, who do not naturally choose to love our neighbors as we love ourselves. As human beings, we are remarkable composites of dust and divinity, continually tempted to exalt one dimension of this mixture to a devastating extreme.

Like sheep, we "nibble" ourselves lost. Isaiah was correct when he wrote, "All we like sheep have gone astray; we have turned every one to his own way" (53:6). We grow up in imperfect families where parents do provoke their children to wrath (see Eph. 6:4). We have the capacity to travel to a far country, while never leaving our hometown, by throwing aside all caution and reason and flaunting the moral law of God and man. We are trapped by an agonizing ambivalence which keeps us in perpetual inner conflict over trying to do right and not do wrong. Admittedly, this is not a pretty picture, but it is our status quo—the immoral mess which involves us all.

Notes

1. Reuel L. Howe, *Man's Need and God's Action* (Greenwich, Conn.: The Seabury Press, 1953), pp. 132-133.

2. Hendrik Kraemer, *The Communication of the Christian Faith* (Philadelphia: The Westminster Press, 1956), pp. 19-20.

3. Clyde T. Francisco, "Genesis," revised, *The Broadman Bible Commentary* (Nashville: Broadman Press, 1973) 1:133.

4. Oscar F. Wilde, *Ballad of Reading Gaol*, Part I, st. vii.

5. Francisco, p. 141.

6. Helmut Thielicke, *How the World Began: Man in the First Chapters of the Bible* (Philadelphia: Muhlenberg Press, 1961), pp. 239-240.

2

Does the Devil Make
Us Do It?

The black entertainer, Flip Wilson, had a popular comedy routine for television built around the personality of his fictitious girl friend, Geraldine. Geraldine could get into all kinds of difficult and impractical situations, only to excuse herself by saying, "The devil made me do it!" Although Flip Wilson and Geraldine made this line quite popular for a while, the kind of moral buck-passing that it points to has been around for a long time.

In a real sense, this kind of coy evasion is as old as the Garden of Eden. God called out, "Where are you?" to Adam in the Garden of Eden, after Adam and Eve had eaten of the forbidden fruit (see Gen. 3:9-13).

Adam replied, "I heard the sound of thee in the garden, and I was afraid, because I was naked; and I hid myself."

And God said, "Who told you that you were naked? Have you eaten of the tree of which I commanded you not to eat?"

To which Adam replied sheepishly, "The *woman* whom thou gavest to be with me, *she* gave me fruit of the tree, and I ate."

Then God said to Eve, "What is this that you have done?"

And Eve replied, "The *serpent* beguiled me, and I ate" (author's italics).

Adam passed the buck to Eve, and Eve in turn passed it on to the serpent. A modern restatement of what Eve said would go something like this: "I gave the forbidden fruit to Adam, but it's really not my fault. You see, the serpent eased up and tricked me into doing it. It's really all his fault! . . . The devil made me do it!"

But does the devil make us do anything? Who, or what, is the devil anyway? Is the devil a serpent? What does he look like? Can we see him? How do we know he is around? Is it possible that the idea of the devil may be just in our imaginations? Is the thought of the devil only an outdated concept from ancient superstition?

In 1941 C. S. Lewis ran a series of letters in a British newspaper which purported to be correspondence between two devils—one retired, and the other just beginning his work on earth. The next year, these weekly articles were published in book form under the title *The Screwtape Letters*. In the almost half century since its release, this book has become a Christian classic in the subtle area of man's encounter with the devil, whom Lewis considered to be quite real.

Lewis made a statement in the Preface to the letters, concerning the reality of the devil and his aides and our understanding of their work: "There are two equal and opposite errors into which our race can fall about the devils. One is to disbelieve in their existence. The other is to believe, and to feel an excessive and unhealthy interest in them. They themselves are equally pleased by both errors and hail a materialist or a magician with the same delight."[1]

Some people today are exalting the role of the devil all out of proportion to his reality. Various satanic cults scattered across the country practice black magic and actually worship the devil. Others of us never give the devil a serious thought. We, consequently, make ourselves more susceptible to his wiles. I have tried to avoid both the error of the materialist and the error of the magician by giving serious, but cautious, thought to the doctrine of the devil and the problem of evil in the world.

How Do You Visualize the Devil?

What image or picture comes to your mind when you think of the devil? Do you see him in some kind of creaturely form? Few, if any of us, would visualize the devil as a small red or green being, resembling a man, but having horns, cloven hoofs, a protruding tail, and carrying a pitchfork. Yet this was a dominant medieval image of the devil. As such, it had more kinship with Faust and Mephistopheles than with the Bible.

I conducted a personal survey to determine where some laypeople are in their current thinking on certain subjects which relate directly to the Christian view of man as sinner. Both men and women were included in my survey. I mailed a questionnaire to one hundred laypersons who are currently serving on representative national and/or state Baptist boards and agencies across the nation. Here are some of the replies which were given concerning the devil.

Some laypeople have little difficulty in defining the idea and role of the devil in our world. A physician wrote straightforwardly, "The devil is a perpetrator of sin. He can be, and is, a tempter." A layman from a middle Western state wrote, "The devil is very much alive in the world, and he is trying to lead us into sin." Another layman declared, "The devil is a spirit which attempts to separate us from God." A chemist from the mid-South wrote, "As the spirit of good leads one to do right, the devil is a spirit of evil, which becomes manifest when we develop a spirit of hatred, etc., instead of love."

Concerning the relationship of the devil to sin, a housewife wrote, "I think of a person with a mean streak in his character or a person who willfully hurts another person as having an evil spirit in his nature, which allows him to do wrong without regard for the consequences. Some people seem almost to have a total pattern of evil in their character makeup, while all of us may, on occasion, yield to temptation, or to a 'devilish spirit' within us, which permits—even urges—us to commit a foolish act."

In contrast to this, some laymen wrote that although they know well the reality of sin and evil, they have some difficulty in conceptualizing the role of the devil. For example, an administrator in the middle West wrote, "Belief in the devil as persona is going out of style, since Satan is not an historical figure in the sense that Jesus was. However, only a naive person would fail to see demonic forces at work in ourselves and in our world."

A layman from an East Coast state wrote: "I don't hear a lot about the devil. I personally think that the devil is unnecessary. The human will is devil enough."

A young mid-South physician wrote with candor: "Whether or not the devil exists, I don't know. Evil certainly does. To me, the real question is who is responsible for my sin(s)! I think that the biblical witness is that *I* am responsible for that sin, and ultimately, for my need of repentance. I believe that the devil, all too often, serves as a convenient scapegoat, allowing us to escape personal responsibility for our sins. To me, this cheapens the meaning of God's forgiveness."

Whether they think they know much or little about the devil, most laypersons readily admit to the reality of sin and evil. Concerning the relationship of the devil and sin, a mid-South CPA summarized concisely as he wrote: "You might say that they are synonymous—one does not exist without the other being present."

With this introductory survey, let us now examine again some of the biblical passages where the devil plays a key role in both influencing man and affecting his behavior. We will, in sequence, review the account of the fall of man in the Garden of Eden, and the epic conflict between Job and his adversary. We will then recall the temptations of Jesus in the wilderness of Judea and also consider some of the general references to the devil in other New Testament books.

The Snake in Eden

As you probably have noted, the story of creation is told from two different perspectives in the first two chapters of Genesis (1:1-4*a;* 2:4*b*-25). The two accounts are complementary, not opposed to one another. You are likely more familiar with Genesis 1. That creation narrative moves from chaos to cosmos, as God created the world and all life in six "days," or six periods of time. The word translated as "day" is synonymous with the Greek word used later in this key New Testament verse: "But do not ignore this one fact, beloved, that with the Lord one day is as a thousand years, and a thousand years as one day" (2 Pet. 3:8; see also Ps. 90:4). On the seventh day, of course, God rested (Gen. 2:2-3).

This account of creation strongly affirms the goodness of God's work. At the end of the sixth day, the writer declared, "God saw *everything* that he had made, and behold, it was *very* good" (1:31, author's italics). God's creation—all of it—was not just *plain* good; it was *very* good. In

Genesis 1:1 to 2:4a, the human race as masculine and feminine persons appeared as the final and crowning event of creation.

In the second account of creation, man as a masculine being is presented as being created earlier in God's plan (2:7). God planted a garden in Eden and placed man there as a caretaker of the garden (v. 8). God caused trees to grow in the garden—trees which were pleasant to the sight and trees which were good for food (v. 9).

The Garden of Eden was a very lovely site. The name *Eden* itself means "pleasant place." When the Septuagint authors later translated the Old Testament from Hebrew into Greek, the word they used for garden was *paradeisos,* that is, paradise. Again, the implication is direct—everything that God made was good.

In fact, the first "not good" thing mentioned in Genesis centers upon the solitude of man. Genesis reports, "Then the Lord God said, 'It is *not good* that the man should be alone; I will make him a helper fit for him'" (v. 18, author's italics). To meet man's need, God created other forms of animal and bird life. But from all of these, "there was not found a helper fit for him" (v. 20).

So God caused a deep sleep to fall upon man. He then took one of man's ribs from his side, and from this rib he fashioned a brand new creature whom man called "Woman." The first recorded poetry in the Bible is man's exclamation when he awoke from his sleep and saw woman (v. 23). If you please, Adam burst into song when he first saw Eve!

Thus the first two chapters in Genesis set forth an idyllic picture of a benevolent God creating from nothing a beautiful, good world. Man and woman were created to enjoy a pleasant life, exercising dominion in the world as the beings more like God than any other creatures which He made.

As the third chapter in Genesis opens, however, we immediately become aware that something in God's beautiful, good world has gone awry. We are introduced to the serpent: "Now the serpent was more subtle than any other wild creature that the Lord God had made" (v. 1).

This statement tells us two specific things about the serpent. First, he is "subtle," that is, clever, crafty, and cunning. Second, he is a part of

God's order of creation. The serpent is presented as a "wild creature," to be sure, but still he is a *creature*, that is, something which God made.

This simple statement is more profound than it may appear. It means that the serpent has no existence apart from God. As we shall see, although the serpent is given no direct connection with the devil as such in the Genesis account, it does become obvious that the serpent is in some way a part of a demonic force which is set at work against what God had intended in creation. The presence of evil in Eden is real, yet this irrational force has being only because God allows it to be. The serpent would have no life if it were not permitted by God.

This means that the Genesis record never assumes any kind of two-headed approach to the matter of good and evil. A thoroughgoing oneness, or monotheism, is dominant in the thought structure of Genesis. Genesis presupposes that there is only one ultimate substance or principle, and that is God. Evil exists, but only as a parasite. Evil can be, but only because there is a greater reality upon which it may feed.

Thus, with great insight and wisdom, the Genesis account declares that the serpent is a part of the created order in which God is the Creator. God is greater than the serpent in every conceivable way. But, how subtle is the serpent—clever, crafty, and cunning! In this guise, he goes to work on man to wreak havoc in God's good world.

It is easy to imagine the serpent choosing an unguarded moment to make his approach to Eve. This is the way the devil still works today. I can surmise that it was "second-cup-of-coffee time," soon after Adam had gone off to work in another area of the garden. You can almost hear the serpent knocking on a tree trunk and suavely saying, "Good morning, Mrs. Eve!"

In whatever way the exact situation developed, the Genesis narrative does indicate that the serpent made his approach to the woman in Eden. There was evidently nothing about the appearance or the approach of the serpent that frightened Eve. There is some reason for thinking that the serpent did not come slithering up to her, since God's later judgment upon the serpent included this sentence:

> Because you have done this,
>   cursed are you above all cattle,

and above all wild animals;
upon your belly you shall go,
and dust you shall eat
all the days of your life (v. 14).

Prior to the encounter with Eve, the serpent may not have been a crawl-ing reptile. He evidently walked right up and spoke directly to her. After all, a *walking* serpent is no more unusual from our point of view than a *talking* serpent.

In one of her books of down-to-earth humor, Jean Kerr tells of a time when her younger son came home from church kindergarten quite down-cast because he had been assigned the role of Adam in the school play. His mother said, "Why, that's just great! That is a lead role in the story of the garden of Eden!"

"I know," the little boy said glumly, "but the *snake* has all the lines!"[2]

Unknowingly, the young boy had affirmed a real truth about evil. The serpent, or the devil, is a wild creature who has, indeed, many "lines."

After they had no doubt exchanged the polite pleasantries of the morn-ing, note what the serpent said to Eve. He actually asked her a question: "Did God say, 'You shall not eat of any tree of the garden'?" (v. 1) The serpent's tone of voice and his body language probably conveyed a mes-sage like this: "Did God *really* tell you you could not eat the luscious fruit of any tree in this beautiful garden? I can't believe He would do a thing like that!"

The woman's initial response was to clarify the serpent's question: "We may eat of the fruit of the trees of the garden; but God said, 'You shall not eat of the fruit of the tree which is in the midst of the garden, neither shall you touch it, lest you die'" (vv. 2-3).

Again, to paraphrase the serpent, his reply conveyed this kind of com-ment: "Did God really tell you that? I still can't believe it! Why, you will not die from eating the fruit of that tree. . . . You see, God's an all right person; but He knows that when you eat of that fruit, some changes will take place. You will see things that you haven't seen before. You will become like God, knowing good and evil. Why, if you ate of that fruit, you would become just as smart as God is!" (see vv. 4-5).

Eve fell for the serpent's clever ploy. She ate of the fruit. Then Adam

ate also. Their eyes were opened, and they became aware of their nakedness. Their sense of nakedness refers to more than just an absence of
clothing. It was more than physical nakedness. In their disobedience,
both man and woman had alienated themselves from God. The wall between them and God also became a barrier isolating each of them from
one another. Loneliness, like a vulture, stalks in the wake of sin, becoming "the specter which haunts unredeemed humanity."[3]

Thus impetuousness and irresponsibility, disobedience and alienation,
sin and guilt invaded the idyllic paradise of Eden. All three of the central
figures in this drama—man, woman, and the serpent—fell under God's
judgment.

In addition to cursing the serpent to be a crawling, slithering, wild
creature, God gave this decree:

> I will put enmity between you and the woman,
>   and between your seed and her seed;
> he shall bruise your head,
>   and you shall bruise his heel (v. 15).

God's promise that the seed of woman will ultimately bruise, or crush,
the head of the serpent, points to the ultimate termination of evil. Thus,
unlike God, evil had a beginning and it will also have an end.

Concerning this key passage, Clyde Francisco offers this helpful com-
ment:

> The declaration of the warfare to come between the serpent and the
> woman has been called the *Protevangelium,* the first gospel, the first good
> news. This was hardly the significance to Adam and Eve. It meant a strug-
> gle to the death between the demonic and the human with little hope of
> survival for either. Some comfort could be found in the certain destruction
> of the demonic (the serpent's head crushed). For the serpent's deadly
> fangs to strike the heel of mankind until it was crushed would normally
> imply death for man also.[4]

Thus the Garden of Eden episode closes, not with a promise of life,
but with an affirmation of the certainty of death. Caught in the folly and
guilt of his own sin, man's life would become a saga of earthbound hope-
lessness.

Nowhere in the Genesis account is the serpent directly identified as the devil. The serpent is an expression of the demonic, but he is never named as the devil. In this respect, the Genesis account is likely reflecting a familiar theme in ancient literature which often connected the realm of evil with serpents. For example, in the Gilgamesh Epic, which is Babylonian literature from the second millennium BC, it is said that a serpent was responsible for man's not attaining eternal life.

Other literature, however, reading Genesis from a later Jewish or Christian point of view, does connect the snake in Eden with the prince of this world, the devil. In the Pseudepigrapha, which is a collection of Jewish writings generally thought to be written during the interbiblical period, the Book of Enoch identifies an angel, Gadreel, who led Eve astray (69:6). From the Apocrypha, a similar collection of Jewish writings, the Wisdom of Solomon includes this statement: "Through the devil's envy death entered the world" (2:24). Some interpreters mark this as an identification of the serpent with the devil.

As the figure of the devil, or the evil one, developed, he came to be recognized as the ultimate source of death. As an almost necessary consequence of this, the devil came to be identified with the serpent in the Garden of Eden (2 Enoch 31:3).

The Christian author of Revelation, writing near the end of the first century in the Christian era, also made this specific connection. John wrote: "And the great dragon was thrown down, *that ancient serpent, who is called the Devil* and Satan, the deceiver of the whole world—he was thrown down to the earth, and his angels were thrown down with him" (12:9, author's italics; see also 20:2).

Satan in the Old Testament

Very little is said in the Old Testament in regard to Satan, or the devil. In fact, William Robinson has written that looking for the devil in the Old Testament is like looking for a needle in a haystack.[5] No direct correlation between the devil and the serpent in Eden was made until the post-Exilic, interbiblical period in Jewish history. The Old Testament canon, as such, did not include any writing in which this connection was made.

Checking an unabridged concordance, you will find that the word *devil* appears only four times in the Old Testament. In each instance, the

Hebrew word form is plural, meaning "devils." Twice this word is a translation of the Hebrew word *sair* (Lev. 17:7; 2 Chron. 11:15), which means "kid" or "goat" or "evil spirit." The Revised Standard Version translated this word in both of these verses as "satyrs."

In the Leviticus reference, as the Jewish sacrificial system and rites of cleansing were being outlined—including the Day of Atonement, God reminded the Israelites that they should no longer slay sacrifices for "satyrs," or "devils" (KJV). In the reference from 2 Chronicles, at the time of the divided kingdom, King Jeroboam in the north deported priests and Levites. These outcast religious leaders went south to Jerusalem and the Kingdom of Judah. Jeroboam replaced these men with bogus priests, who would offer sacrifices in the pagan high places and to the "satyrs," or "devils" (KJV). The word thus referred to a kind of worship that was neither faithful nor pleasing to the Lord God of Israel.

The two other uses of the word *devil* in the Old Testament are translations of the Hebrew word *shed,* which means "destroyer." One of these is found in the song of Moses near the close of the Book of Deuteronomy. The specific reference (32:17) points to the fact that some of the Israelites made sacrifices to "devils" (KJV), or "demons" (RSV), which were not gods.

The other reference is from a similar passage in Psalm 106. In recounting the story of his people from the Exodus to the settlement in Canaan, the psalmist mentioned that, after their arrival in the new land, some of the Israelites sacrificed their sons and daughters to the "devils" (KJV), or the "demons" (RSV) (v. 37). Only four specific references to the devil in the entire Old Testament provide rather sparse documentation for his character.

In like manner, the term *Satan* is found only four times in the Old Testament. In this case, although the number of uses is the same as for the word *devil,* these references offer a bit fuller description of the role and function of this creature. The root Hebrew word from which the name *Satan* is derived means primarily "to obstruct" or "to oppose." When not a proper name, the word is used in the Old Testament to describe obstructing a man's pathway (Num. 22:22) or opposing in a war (1 Sam. 29:4).

In 1 Chronicles, Satan is named as the one who moved David "to number Israel" (21:1). In Psalm 109, Satan is presented in the role of an "accuser" (v. 6), or public prosecutor, to help bring a wicked man to trial. In like manner, the prophet Zechariah wrote of Satan as being an "accuser" (see 3:1). In this role, Satan stands at the right hand of the angel of the Lord. He appears to be something of a public prosecutor in the court of heaven. We know of this role for Satan even more fully, however, from the Book of Job, which is the fourth Old Testament reference to his reality.

In the Book of Job, Satan's role as accuser, or adversary, is spelled out in more detail. As you recall, Job is presented as being a wealthy Middle Eastern sheik who made his money, not in oil, but through his vast herds and/or flocks of animals. He had seven thousand sheep and three thousand camels. Sheep were valuable for both wool and food. Camels were highly prized for both transportation and status. Even today, because of their load-bearing capacity, camels are called the pickup trucks of the desert. He also had five hundred yoke of oxen, and five hundred she-asses. By the standards of that day, Job was a very rich man.

To help oversee this vast retinue, Job had the perfect family—one wife, seven sons, and three daughters. He had the perfect number of sons—seven. Add to that his three daughters, and Job had what was considered to be the all-sufficient family.

By the mind-set of that day, to be so blessed meant that Job had to be a man of great integrity and righteousness. Everything was going his way, with his strong character and his many blessings mutually reinforcing one another.

This picture of domestic bliss, however, was suddenly interrupted by a series of calamities which greatly altered Job's life. As the dramatic story is told, Satan, the adversary, precipitated all of Job's problems.

Like a meeting of the company president and his board of directors, a council meeting was held in heaven, assembling the sons of God with the Lord Himself. Satan was present at the meeting, evidently there as one of the sons of God, that is, as one of the heavenly court of angels.

As this meeting got under way, God asked Satan, "Whence have you come?" (Job 1:7). Satan replied, "From going to and fro on the earth, and from walking up and down on it" (v. 7). In the original language, it is obvious that Satan's answer is actually a play on words with his name. The implication of the answer is that he has been spying on the earth. An espionage role is still befitting to Satan's character as we know him today.

The Lord then asked Satan if he had met Job: "Have you considered my servant Job, that there is none like him on the earth, a blameless and upright man, who fears God and turns away from evil?" (v. 8).

Satan's response is incisive. He asked, "Does Job fear God for nought?" (v. 9). Some commentators think that this is the key nerve of the entire drama and the basic question in the whole book.[6] Why does Job, or anyone else for that matter, worship God? What is Job's motive, or reason, for being a religious person? What's in it for Job?

Satan further pushed his case against Job, which is really an argument opposing God. Satan asserted that God had been overprotective toward Job—putting "a hedge" about him so that he and his family had known no adversity, while experiencing unlimited blessings (v. 10). "But put forth thy hand now, and touch all that he has," Satan chided, "and he [Job] will curse thee to thy face" (v. 11).

In light of such an accusation, God allowed Satan to afflict Job in any way he wished, except bringing him bodily harm. In quick succession, the dramatic story is told of Job's total loss of his children and all of his possessions in various calamities. Yet Job did not curse God. Instead, he worshiped God saying, "The Lord gave, and the Lord has taken away; blessed be the name of the Lord" (v. 21). In all of his trouble, Job neither sinned nor blamed God for his misfortune.

Satan was not silenced easily. A second council meeting was held in heaven. In a similar round of questions, Satan asserted that Job would not remain faithful if he were afflicted with personal, bodily pain. God gave Satan liberty to touch Job with physical maladies, but Job's life was not to be taken. The remainder of the Book of Job is made up of a series of dramatic dialogues through which Job and his would-be friends explore the possible reasons for Job's awful suffering and distress. Satan never reappears in the account.

From the prologue introduction to Job, we can draw certain concluding observations about the role of evil in the world. The presence of evil in our world cannot be denied. Rather than being diffused and abstract, this presence is more often personified and direct. Although evil has existence only because God allows it, personified evil is an affront to God. Evil is against God. Satan has some limited ability to oppose and afflict man. Satan can test, or tempt, man—thereby exposing his hypocrisy and weakness. Satan's influence, although alluring and powerful, is still a role limited by the will and power of God.

From this perspective, it is easy to see how some people would conclude that we as human beings are merely pawns on a chessboard, our lives moved about by the whims and fancies of God and Satan. However, we gain new insights when we consider the role of the devil in the New Testament.

Jesus and the Tempter

One of the reasons that we as modern Christians cannot totally dismiss the idea of the devil is that Jesus Himself knew direct confrontations with him. The Synoptic Gospels refer to the temptation experience of Jesus. Matthew and Luke give fuller accounts of this encounter (Matt. 4:1-11; Luke 4:1-13).

Perhaps significantly, the initial period of temptation came to Jesus immediately following His baptism by John the Baptist in the Jordan River near the vicinity of Jericho. Having known a high moment of divine affirmation at His baptism (Matt. 3:17), Jesus was immediately thrust into a situation in which the mettle of His character was severely tested. Frank Stagg commented that this was not unusual: "Moments of great vision and exaltation are precisely those in which one is most subject to such assault. The higher life is keyed to the potentiality for truth and good, the more open it is to temptation."[7]

Matthew reported that following His baptism, "Jesus was led up by the Spirit into the wilderness to be tempted by the devil" (4:1). The site was likely the wilderness of Judea—the barren, desolate area west of Jericho and the Dead Sea. Visitors to the Bible lands today still see a rugged peak in this area known as the Mount of Temptation. Here Jesus met the devil, Satan, the prince of this world, who deserves the highest degree in the ranks of the hidden persuaders which lure men to destruction.

The encounter of Jesus with the devil was in all probability an inner battle in the sense that it is likely that Jesus did not bodily leave the wilderness area during the entire ordeal. Frank Stagg wrote, "Whatever the meaning of Satan, it is unmistakable that Jesus found the essence of temptation to be deep in the human heart, and it is there that it must be confronted and overcome."[8] This does not mean the temptations were not real. In meeting the devil, Jesus was not shadowboxing. The devil's presence was actual and awesome, as Jesus wrestled with specific issues which would determine His destiny. Having received public acclaim, an opportune moment, and divine approval, what would Jesus now do with the gifts and powers which were His? What kind of Savior would He become?

A careful examination of the three temptations will reveal that they were a strange composite of good and evil. Some of the things which the devil offered were not bad in themselves. They were actually goals which Jesus did want to pursue. The devil's method of reaching these goals, however, left much to be desired. He is the architect of seeking achievement using every shortcut. He also operates on the philosophy that any means is justified to accomplish a worthy goal. In other words, the devil works by the devious principle that the end justifies the means. Let us now carefully examine each of the three temptations.

The Temptation to Turn Stones into Bread

Matthew (4:2) and Luke (4:2) both report that Jesus was in the wilderness fasting for a period of forty days. He became very hungry. At the point of His natural appetite, the devil first approached Jesus. The word translated as "tempted" meant "to test," or "to try."

The round, brown stones in the Judean wilderness bore a striking resemblance to some of the hard-crusted bread baked in Palestinian ovens. Seeking to tempt Jesus at the basic level of His hunger for food, the devil challenged Him to turn some of the rocks into rolls. The tempter said, "If you are the Son of God, command these stones to become loaves of bread" (Matt. 4:3).

The Greek grammar in this sentence is worthy of note. The "if" clause which introduces the devil's assertion is known as a condition of the first class. This grammatical construction assumes that the stated condition is true. We could translate, "Since you are the Son of God. . . ." The subtle challenge of the devil, however, was that Jesus should exercise His power as the Son of God to appease His own hunger and also to prove that what God had said about Him at the time of His baptism was actually true.

The issues at stake in this temptation may be spelled out like this: Would the Son of God turn stones into bread to meet His own personal needs, or would He suffer with the rest of humanity as His incarnation presupposes? Would He be willing to live on a level with those whom He served, or would He use His personal gifts to "feather His own nest"? Would He direct His divine power to be used for satisfying His physical needs, and, in turn, make that the basis for His appeal to other persons? Would He win the hearts of people by filling their stomachs or by challenging their spirits? Ultimately, would He be the *savor* from the bakeshop or the *Savior* from the cross?

The cry of appetite is weighty. The appropriate needs of appetite are legitimate. Yet we should remember that man's appetites are temporal. Many appetites are sensual. Appetites must be disciplined, lest unbridled hunger or passion come to rule and ruin us. Also, we should know that man can satisfy his appetites and still remain famished. The elementary level of appetite is still the first line of defense where the devil makes his attack on us—witness the sins of gluttony, greed, and lust.

Jesus repulsed the tempter with a strong word. "It is written," Jesus said,

> "Man shall not live by bread alone,
> but by every word that proceeds from the mouth of God" (4:4).

It is a simple and profound truth that man's deepest hunger can never be satisfied by bread alone. Augustine of Hippo and Milan echoed this fact in the *Confessions,* when he wrote, "Thou hast created us for thyself, and our hearts are restless until they find rest in thee."

What Jesus in the first temptation would not do for Himself, He did without hesitation when He fed the five thousand in Galilee (John 6:1-5). He miraculously multiplied the "five barley loaves and two fish" (v. 9) so that a multitude was fed. Against the backdrop of this event, Jesus declared, "I am the bread of life" (v. 35). That became one of the most dangerous moments in the early ministry of Jesus. The people suddenly wanted to "take him by force" (v. 15) and make Him their king. The allegiance of the crowd was sparked by the fact that they had been given bread, not because they had come to know Jesus as Savior and Lord. Neither in the wilderness of Judea nor in Galilee did Jesus want to gain loyalty at the primary level of giving bread alone!

The Temptation to Fall from the Temple

The second temptation was more dramatic and public (Matt. 4:5-7). The devil took Jesus to the pinnacle of the Temple. This was a high place on the southeast corner of the Temple area but not exactly like a church steeple. It was actually the highest point in the building from ground surface. The corner overlooked the Kidron Valley, with a view toward the Mount of Olives. This location could have been called "suicide corner" because a drop from this height would have been almost certain death on the rocks below.

In this temptation, Satan encouraged Jesus to throw Himself down from the pinnacle of the Temple and to call upon the angels to bear Him up. Since the Temple corner was a very public place, such a dramatic episode would "wow" many people. The devil was implying that such a dazzling feat would cause the people quickly to become followers of Jesus.

What kind of Messiah would Jesus be? How would He use His gifts to gain a following? Would the Son of God wait patiently until He had won the hearts of men, or would He turn on the glamor and become an expert engineer of consent? Would He appeal to the superficial layer of man's loyalty, never trying to reach the core of his life? Would He be "The Sensation" of Jerusalem or "The Savior" from Galilee?

Jesus' reply (v. 7) indicated His conviction that God is not proved by clever magic nor by sleight of hand tricks. Jesus would take the longer route to win man's allegiance—the way which ultimately led to a cross. Frank Stagg wrote, "Jesus saw that true faith does not try to compel God to act, and true faith cannot be brought about by 'compelling' signs and wonders."[9]

Satan uses this level of temptation in confronting many of us today. The multitalented person is especially vulnerable to this tactic. Shall I use my gifts to dazzle people or to serve people, in Christ's name? Church leaders can be easily tempted in this regard—opting to build their churches around short-term gimmicks of surface evangelism and outreach, rather than following the longer course of nurture and discipleship which results in changed life-styles. Any individual can be tempted to push or force God into action for one's selfish behalf. When any of these snares fall in our way, we should consider their source, as reflected in this temptation of Jesus!

The Temptation to Win the World by False Worship

The third temptation was the climactic one from Matthew's point of view (4:8-10). The devil tempted Jesus by offering to give Him His desired goal: allegiance from all the kingdoms, or peoples, of the world. The price of such loyalty, however, was to be that Jesus would "fall down and worship" Satan (v. 9).

The tempter promised something which he likely could not deliver. This is in character for the hidden persuader—making promises which he cannot keep. Whether or not Satan could deliver, this temptation to Jesus must have been quite strong. The mind-set of many Jewish people in the first century included the popular expectation for a messiah who would give Israel rule over other nations. The Davidic reign and dynasty would be restored, and enlarged.

To consider leadership for the six million Jews scattered throughout the ancient world, in what was often called the Diaspora, must have had an emotional appeal to Jesus. He did feel a keen sense of mission to His own people. Yet He refused to interpret His messianic function in political terms. He chose to be a serving Savior, rather than a reigning Emperor. Jesus' sword is a word of love, not a blade of might. He also affirmed that a moral goal must always be pursued by righteous means. Truth can only be furthered by integrity—not by easy shortcuts or shallow compromises.

We too are tempted to seek our major goals in life by means which are not worthy of Christian consideration. The devil would deceive us into false worship, making promises which he cannot deliver. We must decide whether we will use moral or immoral means to achieve our desired ends in life.

Having been repulsed in all three rounds of this first match with Jesus, the devil then left Him (v. 11). He would be back to tempt Jesus again—at the next "opportune time" as Luke reported (4:13). For the time being, however, the testing time for Jesus had ended. Matthew declared that "angels came and ministered to him" (v. 11).

Other New Testament References to the Devil

From the Words of Jesus

One of the phrases in the model prayer given by Jesus is likely a reference to the devil: "But deliver us from evil" (Matt. 6:13). A definite article occurs in the Greek before the word *evil*. Thus this line may correctly be read, "But deliver us from *the evil one!*"

Jesus also referred to the devil as "the prince" or "the ruler of this world" (John 12:31). In interpreting His parable of the weeds among the wheat (Matt. 13:24-30), Jesus said that "the enemy" who sowed the weeds in the wheat "is the devil" (v. 39). In the parable of the sower, Jesus said that the devil was active in taking away the good seed from the hearts of those who were wanting to believe and be saved (Luke 8:12). In one of the parables in His later ministry, Jesus pointed to the final destruction "prepared for the devil and his angels" (Matt. 25:41).

When Peter would have prevented Jesus from returning to Jerusalem where His death seemed imminent, Jesus, in essence, told Peter that he was talking like the devil. He said to Peter, "Get behind me, Satan! You are a hindrance to me; for you are not on the side of God, but of men" (Matt. 16:23).

From the Writings of Paul

Paul referred to the "God of peace" who "will soon crush Satan under your feet" in closing his letter to the Romans (16:20). In writing the Thessalonians, Paul indicated that "Satan hindered" him in his efforts to see them again (1 Thess. 2:18). In his second letter to the church at

Thessalonica, Paul referred to the "activity of Satan" in the coming of
the lawless one (2 Thess. 2:9).

Two of Paul's best known references to the devil are found in Ephesians. He counseled these friends to control their anger so that they
would "give no opportunity to the devil" (4:27). He also urged the
Ephesians to "put on the whole armor of God, that you may be able to
stand against the wiles of the devil" (6:11). The word "wiles" means sly
tricks, or beguiling deceits.

From the Writings of Peter

In the closing counsel of the first letter which bears his name, Peter
gave an impassioned plea relative to the devil: "Be sober, be watchful.
Your adversary the devil prowls around like a roaring lion, seeking some
one to devour. Resist him, firm in your faith, knowing that the same
experience of suffering is required of your brotherhood throughout the
world" (1 Pet. 5:8-9).

Peter's simile to describe the devil was graphic. He pictured the devil
to be like a roaring lion prowling around, seeking to devour someone.
His imagery may have been borrowed from Psalm 22:13. If you have
ever visited a zoo at feeding time, you likely have heard the roar of lions.
A lion roars to express his hunger. Thus, Peter described the devil as
being like a roaring lion, gripped by the rage of hunger, prowling the
earth seeking to devour someone.

Peter urged his friends in Asia Minor to stand up against this lethal
influence which would try to destroy them. Using an imperative verb
form, Peter wrote: "Resist him" (1 Pet. 5:9). The Greek word here liter-
ally means "to stand against." Peter knew that rolling over and playing
dead was not sufficient opposition to put the devil to flight. Such coward-
ice never wins against the devil. Only a courage which takes a positive,
aggressive stand is able to "quench all the flaming darts of the evil one"
(Eph. 6:16).

Thus We Conclude

However much we may dislike the idea of the devil and all his associates, we must conclude that there are many references in the Bible which

point to his actual existence. Our study in this chapter should lead us to these affirmations about the devil:

1. He is not like any of the crude, or grotesque, figures which have sprung up about him in various eras of history.

2. He is not coequal with God and independent of Him.

3. He is not an illusion; he is real.

4. He is the personification of evil—subtle and personal.

5. He is a liar, a tempter, an accuser, a deceiver—cunningly deceptive in his ability to appear as an angel of light when actually he is the prince of darkness.

6. He is a parasite—having no existence apart from the goodness of God.

7. He affects, but he does not determine man's moral behavior. The devil can and will tempt us to do evil, but he cannot make us do it!

Notes

1. C. S. Lewis, *The Screwtape Letters* (Chicago: Lord and King Associates, Inc., 1976), p. 9.

2. Jean Kerr, *The Snake Has All the Lines* (New York: A Crest Book, 1962), p. viii.

3. Cuthbert A. Simpson, "Exegesis of Genesis," *The Interpreter's Bible* (New York: Abingdon Press, 1952) 1:506.

4. Clyde T. Francisco, "Genesis," Revised, *The Broadman Bible Commentary* (Nashville: Broadman Press, 1973) 1:131.

5. William Robinson, *The Devil and God* (New York: Abingdon-Cokesbury Press, 1945), p. 48.

6. John D. W. Watts, "Job," *The Broadman Bible Commentary* (Nashville: Broadman Press, 1971) 4:38.

7. Frank Stagg, "Matthew," *The Broadman Bible Commentary* (Nashville: Broadman Press, 1969) 8:99.

8. Ibid., p. 97.

9. Ibid., p. 98.

3

What is Sin?

Have you heard someone mention a certain embarrassing or compromising situation in his life and then quickly excuse the matter by saying, "... but I really wasn't sinning!"? A rather typical teenage boy, trying to explain to his parents an episode of unwise behavior on his part, finally concluded—"But what I did was no *big* sin! . . . *Nobody's perfect!*"

A patient in the maximum security ward of a state mental hospital told a young chaplain intern the series of events which led to his being hospitalized. The road down finally culminated in another person being killed. The patient concluded his story by saying, "I know what my file down in the main office says about me, but that's really *not me*. I'm not a killer!"

Such statements from real life cause us to ask these basic questions: What is sin? What kind of reality are we pointing to when we use this three-letter word? Can we arrive at a working definition of sin?

Definitions of Sin from Representative Laymen

In the previous chapter, I referred to a survey questionnaire which I mailed to one hundred representative Christian laypersons, requesting input and suggestions from them for writing this book. One of the questions included in this personal survey was phrased simply like this: "How do you define sin?" The responses were varied, insightful, and right to the point.

Several of these laypersons defined sin primarily in terms of man's relationship to God. For example, a retired chemist wrote: "Sin is any action or thought on my part that is contrary to God's wishes for me. I must believe that whatever God wants me to do is best for me. He does not lay down laws of conduct that result in harm to me or to any other person who obeys them." Another layman wrote, "Sin is anything that separates *me* from God."

Other laypeople marked out sin basically in terms of breaking God's law. A career homemaker-businesswoman defined sin "as a transgression of God's law, especially the breaking of the Ten Commandments as given by God through Moses." A career farmer said straightforwardly, "I think of sin as a disobedience of God's law." A mid-South CPA enlarged the idea of breaking the law in his definition: "Sin is the breaking of the Ten Commandments, the Lord's eleventh commandment, or the breaking of city, state, or national laws which are not in contradiction to biblical teachings."

Other laymen defined sin essentially in terms of its individual and/or social implications. They tended to view sin in terms of how it affects both the sinner and other people. A perceptive Christian woman wrote: "Sin is a foolish act. It may be doing something hastily which may harm some other person, or it may be neglecting to do something which could prevent hurt to self or other people. At first I thought I might answer that sin is breaking any of the Ten Commandments. As a Christian, however, I would say that sin is committing an act that is contrary to the teachings of Christ. But to simplify, one sins if he or she willfully or carelessly does something which causes hurt to come to another person or himself."

A retired manufacturer of agricultural equipment thinks of sin primarily in terms of "mistreatment or unfairness to one's fellow man. This could be in business deals, in excessive self-indulgence which results in family neglect and abuse, in failing to aid those persons who are in real need so that they are not encouraged to try to help themselves."

A Middle Western administrator in higher education also shared this view of sin, as he wrote: "Sin is that combination of collection of forces in the world which prevent the realization of the kingdom of God. Sin has both individual and social dimensions, and will not be overcome until both I and the whole external world have been redeemed and purified."

Still other laymen defined sin more in terms of an inner attitude than an outward act. Reflecting perhaps one of the skills of his profession, a radiologist gave this view of sin: "As a Christian, I believe sin is basically a problem of attitude and man's integrity in his relationship with God. Sin becomes a problem of attitude because proper fellowship with God is necessary after we commit ourselves to the Lordship of Christ. This requires obedience to Him, and includes the desire to avoid actions and ideas that are in conflict with God's righteousness and holiness."

A forest products industrialist reflected a similar opinion, and also tied his understanding of sin with breaking the law: "One dictionary defines sin as 'the breaking of religious or moral law.' I think this is how sin is commonly understood. There is no doubt in my mind that the religious 'leaders' of His day saw Jesus as a sinner, because He certainly broke religious law, tradition, and custom. . . . But I am inclined to think that sin is primarily a manifestation of selfishness. I see myself in sin when I depart from a servant relationship with God, which is always. I do not understand why I, or others, do this, since I think life would be much less complicated and much more enjoyable if we were all good servants of God all the time."

Finally, a retired lumberman wrote his definition of sin in this way: "I think of sin as any act, or failure to act, on one's part that moves the individual farther from God and his fellowman. I do not think of sin as a breach of code, or a breaking of rules of conduct. I rather think of sin in terms of aims, purposes, and attitudes. Jesus Himself said, 'As a man thinketh in his heart. . . .'"

In the preface to this volume, I made reference to Karl Menninger's book, *Whatever Became of Sin?* Dr. Menninger defines sin in this manner:

> Sin is transgression of the law of God; disobedience of the divine will; moral failure. Sin is failure to realize in conduct and character the moral ideal, at least as fully as possible under existing circumstances; failure to do as one ought towards one's fellow man. . . . Sin has a willful, defiant, or disloyal quality; *someone* is defied or offended or hurt. The willful disregard or sacrifice of the welfare of others for the welfare or satisfaction of the self is an essential quality of the concept *sin*. . . . Sin traditionally implies guilt, answerability, and by derivation, responsibility. For many it implies confession, attrition, reparation, repentance, forgiveness, atonement. . . I shall proceed on the assumption that the word sin *does*

imply these corollaries and that I at least find the corollaries acceptable in principle.[1]

Definitions of Sin in the Old Testament

In the Bible, sin is treated very gravely. Human sin is no casual concern or joking matter. Sin often is seen as a crucial matter of life or death. One commentator describes the biblical viewpoint on sin with these strong words:

> The Bible takes sin in dead seriousness. Unlike many modern religionists, who seek to find excuses for sin and explain away its seriousness, . . . the writers of the Bible had a keen awareness of its . . . tragedy. They knew that apart from God, man is a lost sinner, unable to save himself or find true happiness.[2]

Biblical terminology for sin is rich and graphic. The poets and prophets of Israel were not at a loss for words in setting forth their understanding of sin. As in the case for much of the theological language in the Bible, the terms for sin came more from the marketplace than the worship center. The primary Old Testament words for sin have a this-worldly character about them which gives a sense of vitality and bite which could come in no other way.

Three Primary Old Testament Words for Sin

The Old Testament word translated *sin* comes from a Hebrew stem which means "to miss," or "to fail." At times in the Old Testament, this word is used with just this basic meaning. For example, in describing the accuracy of the left-handed Benjaminites with their slings, the writer said that "every one could sling a stone at a hair, and not *miss*" (Judg. 20:16, author's italics). That was real sharp shooting!

This same word was used to describe missing the mark in matters of morality. As such, it referred primarily to an accidental error, such as an archer unintentionally missing the bull's eye, on a target. Some moral and spiritual failures were seen to be just this kind of accidental, unintended sin.

Another Hebrew term referring to wrong behavior is often translated "iniquity." This word pictures conscious or intentional misbehavior. A person does not commit "iniquity" accidentally. The verb form of this word means "to twist," or "to pervert." Sometimes the term is used in an actual physical sense. When describing God's forthcoming judgment on the nations, Isaiah wrote:

> Behold, the Lord will lay
>> waste the earth and make it desolate,
>> and he will *twist* its surface and scatter
>>> its inhabitants (24:1, author's italics).

When applied to our moral lives, to commit iniquity means that we have twisted, or distorted, God's intended will and way for some important area of our lives. To use a commonplace expression of today, to commit iniquity means that we have morally "bent ourselves out of shape!"

A third term used in the Old Testament to describe human error is translated "transgression." This word refers to human action which must be seen as open defiance against God. Of these three terms, *transgression* is the most profound Hebrew word for *sin*. More than an accidental mistake, or a twisted distortion, transgression indicates open revolt, or rebellion, against God. It points to acts of willful disobedience. At times, this Hebrew term describes a revolt among the nations (see 1 Kings 12:19; Amos 1:3), but usually this word refers to action which was directed against God in overt defiance to His rule.

All three of these words are used in the confession of sin set forth in Psalm 51. Many students consider this psalm to be the most intensely personal of the seven penitential psalms in the Psalter. The title of this psalm assigns it to the Davidic collection. We have traditionally interpreted the psalm as a penitent cry from the heart of King David after his sins of lust, adultery, lying, and murder in relationship to Bathsheba and Nathan. David cried:

> Have mercy on me, O God, according to thy steadfast love;
>> according to thy abundant mercy blot out my *transgressions*.
> Wash me thoroughly from my *iniquity*,
>> and cleanse me from my *sin!* (vv. 1-2, author's italics).

The psalmist knew he had missed God's mark for his life. He had intentionally twisted out of shape God's will for his life. He had also lived in open revolt against God's revealed way for his life. With great pangs of conscience, he admitted who he was—a sinner in deed and truth!

Other Old Testament Words for Sin

Still other words in the Old Testament are used to describe sin. One Hebrew term refers to what we might term "sins of ignorance." As unknowing sheep wander, or stray, from the flock and the shepherd into danger, so people may ignorantly wander into the clutches of sin (see Isa. 53:6). Ezekiel used this word on one occasion to describe the sin of the Israelites: "But the Levites who went far from me, going *astray* from me after their idols when Israel went *astray,* shall bear their punishment" (44:10, author's italics).

Another Old Testament term for sin refers to the accidental or ruthless violation of that which was considered holy. The word carries the idea of pollution, or profaneness. Ezekiel used this word in lamenting for the king of Tyre:

> By the multitude of your iniquities,
>> in the unrighteousness of your trade
>> you *profaned* your sanctuaries;
> so I brought forth fire from the midst of you;
>> it consumed you (28:18, author's italics).

Although the specific word as such is not used, the death of Uzzah while moving the ark of the Lord probably reflects this idea of sin (1 Chron. 13:9-10). That which was holy had been profaned, or polluted, by Uzzah's inadvertent touch.

The language of the Old Testament also contrasts good and bad as distinct qualities. Bad is the opposite of good in terms of the productivity of the land (Num. 13:19), in terms of the appropriateness or inappropriateness of an animal given as an offering to the Lord (Lev. 27:9-13) or in terms of the moral rightness or wrongness of specific human behavior (2 Sam. 13:20-22). Thus bad can be unproductive, inappropriate, or wrong action.

Basic New Testament Words for Sin

The terminology for sin is prominent and extensive in the New Testament. In many ways, the Hebrew words for *sin* in the Old Testament find their counterparts in the Greek words for *sin* in the New Testament. The continuity between the Old and the New Covenants can be affirmed in terms of the language which is used to describe sin. The New Testament clearly recognizes the all-pervading presence of sin, and the problem or predicament which sin creates for man.

In one important regard, however, a sharp contrast can be made between the Old and New Testament views of sin. S. J. De Vries described this distinction:

> All the old terms and concepts are . . . in the New Testament, but deepened and strangely transformed. The one factor which makes this great difference is the work of Jesus Christ. He provides something which the saints of the Old Testament yearned for but could never find: real and certain victory over sin. The doctrine of sin in the New Testament is dominated by the assurance that Christ has come to conquer it. Thus, whatever is said to emphasize sin's deadliness and seriousness serves to magnify the greatness of the salvation from sin which Christ has obtained.[3]

The moving New Testament account of man's redemption from sin is the subject of *God's Work of Salvation,* volume 8, in this particular doctrinal series. But at this point, we will examine more carefully the basic New Testament terminology for sin.

By far the most frequently used New Testament word for *sin* is the Greek word, *hamartia,* which means "a missing of the mark." The carry-over from Hebrew thought should be obvious. In classical Greek, this word indicates the missing of a target, or the missing of a road. It could, thus, refer to taking a wrong turn. Behind such action, there can be either accidental intellectual error or moral fault. In the New Testament, this word occasionally describes man's wrong behavior against his fellowman, but primarily the word refers to wrong action toward God.

Another Greek word for *sin* in the New Testament is *hamartōlos,* which could be used as a noun or an adjective. It is usually translated "guilty," or "wicked." The word indicates a person of notoriously bad morals, such as a tax collector or harlot (Matt. 9:10-11; Luke 7:37; Jas. 4:8; 5:20). In the mind set of that day, these two professions represented the lowest and most degrading forms of work which a man or woman could pursue. In the language of the Pharisees, this word described those persons who would not follow their various rituals (Matt. 15:2; Luke 11:37-38). Occasionally, this word in the New Testament designates the Gentiles as a group not known to God (Matt. 26:45; Luke 6:32-34). In a more spiritual sense, the word is applied to people who were outside of Christ and under God's condemnation (Mark 8:38; Rom. 5:8). It is also at times a self-designation for those persons who were under the conviction of guilt (Luke 5:8; 18:13; 1 Tim. 1:15).

Other New Testament words for *sin* include the term *parabasis,* which was usually translated "transgression." As its counterpart in the Old Testament, this word refers to a deliberate breach of the law, or a conscious lapse into immoral behavior. In contrast to such misbehaving which was done with one's eyes wide open, the Greek terms *agnoia* and *agnoēma* describe sins which are committed "unknowingly," or in "ignorance." It is this basic Greek word stem which gives us our word *agnostic.*

Perhaps the strongest theological word for *sin* in the New Testament is the term *asebeia,* which can be translated "sacrilege," "impiety," or "ungodliness." This word designates human behavior which is primarily an affront, or an insult, to God. Paul used this word in Romans and the Pastoral Letters. It is also found in 1 and 2 Peter, and in Jude.

Asebeia describes sin which is an offense to God in distinction from human action which primarily involves unjust, or unethical, behavior toward another human being. Wrongdoing toward other persons is conveyed by the Greek term *adikia,* which means "unrighteousness," or "injustice." The root stem idea for righteousness is "straightness." Thus, unrighteous action is behavior which is not straight or fair.

Still another New Testament term for *sin* is the Greek word *anomia,* which means "lawlessness" (John 3:4-6). This word, or one of its derivatives, is used to describe attitudes or actions which held the law in contempt. Such a lawless person tries to live as though there were no laws for life. The word can refer to a conscious contempt for the law, in which a person blatantly disobeyed. Or the term can describe someone who sinned, unaware or ignorant of what he was doing. Obviously in this latter case, such ignorance is not bliss!

Thus We Conclude

What can we conclude from this review of Old and New Testament words used to describe the reality which we call sin? The American theologian Reinhold Niebuhr, midway through this century, wrote this summary statement on the biblical definition of sin:

> The Bible defines sin in both religious and moral terms. The religious dimension of sin is man's rebellion against God, his effort to usurp the place of God. The moral and social dimension of sin is injustice. The ego which falsely makes itself the centre of existence in its pride and will-to-power inevitably subordinates other life to its will and thus does injustice to other life.[4]

From this word study, we may conclude that sin is the result of man's failure to live up to his God-ordained potential. It is a missing of the mark that God had purposed for human life. The word points to an accidental or intentional twisted perversion of God's will. Sin can also be rank rebellion against God.

The reality to which sin points may involve sexual immorality, but its total scope is far wider than this single area alone. Sin involves the whole gamut of man's capacity for relationship with God and with other people. Sin is more than just something we do. We may sin in attitude as well as in action. Sin is *bad* attitudes and behavior, in contrast to *good* attitudes and behavior. In contrast to righteousness, which is "straight" living, sin is unrighteousness—a life-style marked by crookedness and not-straight living. Sin brings defilement and pollution to that which is holy and clean. Whether we sin with deliberate malice or in the ignorance of innocence, the end result of sin brings destruction and death.

Notes

1. Karl Menninger, *Whatever Became of Sin?* (New York: Hawthorn Books, Inc., 1973), pp. 18-20.

2. S. J. De Vries, "Sin, Sinners," *The Interpreter's Dictionary of the Bible* (New York: Abingdon Press, 1962) R—Z:361.

3. Ibid., pp. 370-71.

4. Reinhold Niebuhr, *The Nature and Destiny of Man* (New York: Charles Scribner's Sons, 1949), p. 179.

4

What Does Sin "Look Like" in Real Life?

One of my close friends during seminary days was a fellow student who had graduated from the United States Naval Academy in Annapolis, Maryland. After completing his college career as a midshipman, my friend had worked during World War II with the Department of the Navy in Washington, D.C. His older brother was also in military service with the United States Army at this time.

These brothers had had wartime assignments which necessitated their traveling to various parts of the country. As a rule, they travelled on commercial carriers. Several times they happened to be at the same bus terminal, train station, or airport. In such circumstances, they developed a comic routine for greeting one another.

The brother who first noticed his relative nearby would walk over, slap him on the shoulder, and begin, "Say, don't I know you?"

The other brother would reply, "Well, you do look a bit familiar. . . . Where're you from?"

The first man would say, "I'm from Oklahoma."

The second man would respond, "I'm from Oklahoma too!"

The first brother would add, "Where did you live in Oklahoma?"

The second brother would answer, "Oh, I grew up in 'the city.'"

"Well, that's interesting! I grew up in 'the city' too! . . . Where did you live there?"

"My family lived out on the north side of the city."

"Would you believe it! My family lived out on the north side also. Where did you live out there?"

"We lived on Pratt Street."

"We lived on Pratt Street too! What was your house number?"

"We lived at 4508 Pratt Street."

"Why, that's where we lived too!"

Then both young men would exclaim "Brother!" and hug one another enthusiastically.

One evening in a crowded bus station in the southeastern part of the country, these two brothers accidentally bumped into each other and went through this routine. A lady, who appeared to be in her sixties, heard all of this conversation, having no idea of what was actually taking place.

When the two men reached their climactic moment of greeting, it was more than the older woman could take. She suddenly rose to her feet and emphatically walked away, muttering disgustedly, "Can you imagine that! Didn't even recognize his own brother!"

Failure to recognize someone or something with which we should be familiar is not always so humorous. Such failure is always frustrating, and it can sometimes be quite dangerous. Failure to read highway signs correctly at an interstate cloverleaf can result in needless extra mileage and loss of precious time. Failure to see a stop sign at a major intersection can result in a bad accident and serious injury. Failure to see a rattlesnake coiled beside a fallen log in the forest can result in a venomous bite which carries the possibility of death.

The definitions of sin given in the previous chapter are precise and correct. They are illustrative and helpful in gaining an understanding of what sin is. As such, however, they could be considered somewhat vague and abstract. For example, how do we know when we miss the mark? Where is the mark located? Who put it there? When is human behavior an act of rebellion? What is the standard which determines when individual action is obedient and when it is rebellious? We can clearly determine whether a stick is straight or crooked, but how is human behavior measured in this regard? What guidelines tell us when a person is "living straight," and when he or she is "bent out of shape"?

To gain a clearer view of what sin is, we need additional information. The Bible is quite helpful at this point. The Bible enables us to see what sin looks like in the real world.

The Description of Sin in the Law of Moses

In many respects, the epitome of Old Testament morality is found concisely summarized in the Ten Commandments. These commands were given by God to Moses on Mount Sinai, as the Israelites were en route from Egypt to Canaan in the great Exodus (Ex. 19:1-6; 20:1-17). The Sinai experience was a real watershed in the transformation of the struggling refugees into a new fledgling nation. From that general area, God had called Moses to return to Egypt and to give direction to the Exodus. Also in that general area, Israel entered into a new covenant relationship with God.

A few years ago, front-page headlines in newspapers around the world were telling of the establishment of a "Sinai Pact" which stopped the Israeli-Egyptian war which was then in progress. Names and places like these were much in the news at that time—Sadat, Rabin, Kissinger, Suez Canal. The drama of that time reminded many of us of a still yet greater drama which was once enacted near this immediate area on the Sinai Peninsula in the Middle East. Names and places in that script read like this: Moses, Ramses II, Jethro, Red Sea.

Internal evidence in the Bible (Ex. 19:1; Num. 10:11-12) indicates that the stay of the Israelites at Sinai lasted almost one year. The significance of what took place there can hardly be overestimated. Pointing to the pivotal role of the Sinai experience, Roy Honeycutt declared, "All before Sinai is prelude; all that follows is postlude."[1]

The key word *exodus* occurs only at this point in the entire book named Exodus (19:1). Translated as "gone forth out" in both the King James Version and the Revised Standard Version, the original word is *exodus*. This descriptive word not only became the title of an Old Testament book but also came to commemorate the most decisive event in Israel's history.

The "wilderness of Sinai" (v. 2) does not mean wilderness in the sense of being a jungle of dense forests and undergrowth. A better translation of the word is "desert." If you have seen news films of this area, you know how dry and desolate it remains today. In the midst of the desert and before the mountain of God, Israel encamped, never thereafter to be quite the same.

The narrative content tells of God's invitation to the people to meet Him at Sinai, to hear and obey His voice, and to enter into covenant relationship with Him (vv. 4-6). Responding to God's initiative, Moses went up into the mountain where God spoke to him. God asked Moses to remind the people of what He had just done. He had destroyed their Egyptian captors, and He had led them to this point in their trek with the same care as a mother eagle who bears her young on her wings (v. 4).

With this tremendous feat accomplished, God made His proposal to Israel more explicit. He said, "If you will obey my voice and keep my covenant . . ." (v. 5). "Obey my voice" probably points to the Ten Commandments—often called "the ten words"—which are just a bit later introduced with this line: "And God spoke *all these words*" (Ex. 20:1, author's italics). The word "keep" means to have charge of, as a garden, or as property in trust. It can also mean to retain, as in storing food or to meet one's obligations. All of these shades of meaning contribute to the idea of "keeping" the covenant.

Such obedient loyalty on Israel's part would bring the nation into a unique relationship with Yahweh: "You shall be my own possession among all peoples . . . and you shall be to me a kingdom of priests and a holy nation" (vv. 5-6). These phrases certainly mean that Israel was to be supremely dedicated to the Lord. They also may carry the idea that Israel was to fulfill a role of mediator for the rest of the world. This idea is closely related to what Christians mean today when we say "the priesthood of the believers"—that every person within the covenant community is a priest before God (1 Pet. 2:9). This was the message which God commissioned Moses to tell the people.

According to the custom of that day, the covenant between God and Israel was of the suzerainty type. This word describes a promise or agreement made between two parties of unequal status. It was the kind of covenant which was made between a king and his subjects. Certain demands were set forth in this kind of covenant that the lesser party in the covenant was obliged to fulfill. The demand of the covenant at Sinai between God and Israel is stated in what we know as the Ten Commandments, or the Decalogue (Ex. 20:1-17).

In the preface I referred to Archie Bunker's comments about the Ten Commandments. "My religion is simple," said Archie. "The Ten Commandments, that's my religion. I call 'em the 'Big Ten' and I keep 'em too." In one respect, Archie was right. The Ten Commandments are a kind of "Big Ten"—more profoundly so than Archie, and many of us, may realize. In spite of his lavish praise, however, Archie would have been hard pressed to say why he thought the Ten Commandments are so great. If asked, he would probably have replied casually, "Why, . . . any Dingbat knows that!" and let it go.

When we smile at Archie, we may be laughing at ourselves. How much do you know about the Ten Commandments? Could you name all of them—in order? Do you know why they are listed as they are? What would you say to someone who argued that the Commandments are outdated and obsolete? Do you think the Commandments are too negative for our day of positive affirmation?

As we endeavor to get a picture of what sin is like in the real world, we do well to look carefully at the Ten Commandments. They do form the basis of moral obligation which underlies the Sinai covenant between God and those who would be His people—both in Moses' day and in our own day.

The Ten Commandments are both laws for living and living law. They are for all people everywhere because they deal with the very essence of life. They are basic to good living, and no person can escape them. They continue to play a crucial role in our discovery of the good life on this earth. William Barclay has said that the Commandments are not the end of all things, but they are a significant beginning. They represent the very principles of self-limitation and self-discipline without which it is impossible for people to live together in peace with God and with themselves.[2]

Barclay wrote a very fine summary of the all-inclusive scope of the Ten Commandments:

> It must be said that this code inculcates two basic things—it demands *reverence for God* and *respect for man*. The majesty of God and the rights of human personality are alike conserved. This is intensely significant, for it is of the very essence of Judaism, and of the very essence of Christianity, that both have a two-directional look. They look both to God and to man. . . . No man dare say that he loves God, unless he also loves his fellow man; and no man can really and truly love his fellow man, unless he sees that the true value of a man lies in the fact that he is a child of God.

Without the manward look religion can become a remote and detached mysticism in which a man is concerned with his own soul and his own vision of God and nothing more. Without the Godward look a society can become a place in which, as in a totalitarian state, men are looked on as things and not as persons. Reverence for God and respect for man can never be separated from each other.[3]

So, rather than being silent relics of a past era, or footnotes in the history of Western culture, the Commandments still speak today with a blunt, honest counsel which cannot be surpassed or ignored. Joy Davidman has well said: "On the thunderstone of the Tablets. . . . Western civilization has built its house. If the house is tottering today we can scarcely steady it by pulling the foundation out from under."[4]

In addition to all that has been presented, we need to understand the spirit in which these laws were given by God to Moses and the Israelites. Although the majesty of God is strongly affirmed by the Decalogue, the dominate mood of the Commandments is not despotic. God was not reflecting an arbitrary attitude which in essence declared, "I'm bigger and better than you are. This is the way life has got to be lived, *because I said so!*"

Instead of reflecting such a rigorous dogmatism, the Ten Commandments reveal God's desire to let people know in advance how best to live. The Sinai experience was awesome; it was also warmly personal. God was saying to Moses and the Israelites something like this: "I am your Creator and Deliverer. Human life was my idea. You are an expression of my purpose and design. As the author of life, *I want to let you in on the secret of how life will go best for you.* I don't want you to wander in the darkness of ignorance. I want you to know the very best way in which to find the fullness of life which I have planned for you. Here it is, in ten concise statements!"

The Decalogue is an expression of God's law, the Torah, but a strong dimension of God's grace and love is in these statements of His law. This truth should become more evident as we examine each Commandment in further detail. Such a concept of the Decalogue means that sin—in addition to being a breaking of God's law—is also a violation of His love.

Although there is a slight variation in the way some church groups have numbered the Ten Commandments, the predominant arrangement places the first four Commandments on table 1, which has primary concern with man's relationship to God. The last six Commandments compose table 2, which deals primarily with a person's life in relationship to other people. The pivotal connecting link between these two tables is the Fifth Commandment, which has to do with the home and family. Much data has been amassed by the social scientists of our day, affirming that the home and nuclear family are where we learn our most indelible lessons about both ourselves and God.

Let us examine these two tables of the law more carefully and note the specific commands which each of them contains. Our picture of what sin looks like in the real world should become more sharply focused as we see what the Decalogue demands.

Reverence for God

1. The First Commandment declares that a person's good life on earth begins with God: "You shall have no other gods before me" (Ex. 20:3). In a real sense, God told Moses and the Israelites that He had earned the right to be first in their love and loyalty. He had brought them out of bondage in Egypt (v. 2). As both their Creator and their Deliverer, God could legitimately request their supreme allegiance.

This command is actually a call to worship. Our word *worship* comes from the old Anglo-Saxon stem, "worth-ship." To worship is, thus, to recognize true worth and value. When we worship God, we find in Him our center of highest worth. Such priority is rightfully God's. But it is also best for us as His creatures. Just as a wheel will be "out-of-round" when it is off center, our lives will not run smoothly when God is not at the center of our living. The sin in real life from the first command is thus the conscious, or unconscious, attitude which allows God to be put in second place—or in a lesser place—in our lives and the resultant distress which comes from such misplaced loyalty.

Many of us are still searching for a center for our identity. Where have we placed God's kingdom and His righteousness in our scale of values? What does our checkbook, for example, reveal in this regard? When budgeting our time to meet increasing pressures, what kind of priority does God receive in our choices?

2. The Second Commandment addresses the continual temptation for persons to fashion gods in their own likeness: "You shall not make for yourselves a graven image" (Ex. 20:4). This command is at the same time one of the most *simple* and one of the most *subtle* in the Decalogue. Not often, if ever, have we seen someone bowing down in worship to a god made of wood, metal, or stone. Such graven-image gods, however, may sneak up on us in the form of a special place, an exalted person, a well-oiled cultural pattern, a specific mind-set.

Having no statue of Buddha on our mantels does not automatically mean that our houses are free of idols. An idol is anything that comes between us and our relationship to the living God. We can thus "idolize" people, places, ideas, and countless other things. We are constantly tempted to make a god in our image, rather than live in the knowledge and faith that mankind was made in the image of God. The true God speaks, hears, and acts in our lives. The "no-gods" are speechless, deaf, and incapable of action.

What's the shape of our idols? Since idols may take many forms, no one can say glibly, "Well, at least I keep the Second Commandment. I'm not an idolater!" Many of us have discovered that *mental* images can be just as rigid and fixed as *metal* images. Certain mind-sets can seem to be made of steel. Have you ever tried to change a person's mind who held ungodly views on race, money, sex, or war? Or again, from some religious behavior which we are seeing today, we are forced to ask, "When does a spiritual leader cease to be a 'guru' and become an 'idol'"?

The sin in real life for this command relates to the subtle ways we can allow another person, or images of any kind, to assume a "god-role" in our lives. For example, in what respect do you think that "the American way of life" or "white supremacy" or "black power" can become idolatrous culture images?

3. The Third Commandment calls for people who are in covenant with God to take His name in earnest: "You shall not take the name of the Lord your God in vain" (Ex. 20:7).

In one sense, this Commandment may have been followed more faithfully than any other word in the Decalogue. So sacred did God's name become in later Jewish thought that it was considered too holy for anyone to speak. Since the written Hebrew words had no vowels in them until about AD 1000, the vowel portion of the name was actually lost. Today, as best we can determine, the name Israel called God was "Yahweh."

In the Bible, the name of an individual was generally descriptive of the person, his position, some circumstances affecting him, or a hope entertained concerning him. A person's name was the index to his character. In His initial encounter with Moses, God revealed Himself to Israel by a new name (Ex. 3:13-15). God's name was an essential part of His personality. The very mention of His name called forth the power and character of His whole person.

Only in light of this pervading atmosphere of holiness and respect can we begin to understand the Third Commandment. To use God's name falsely was to violate His entire being. Any tendency toward profanity was taboo for the faithful Jew. How much more should the same be true for the Christian! Cursing is a bad habit. Rather than an evidence of strength and toughness, it indicates carelessness, lack of respect, and plain ignorance. For want of a better vocabulary, we express the whole range of emotional reactions in our slang, which all too often profanes God's holy name

The sin in breaking this Commandment is not just speaking God's name "in vain," that is, empty it of all appropriate meaning. The even greater sin is taking His name carelessly or flippantly, stripping it of its power by our own inappropriate actions. Those of us who are New Testament believers have taken the name of Christ as part of our identity. We are called "Christians," that is, "Christ-ones." Jesus may sometimes see our behavior and wish, "Either you should change your conduct, or change your name!"

Concerning the meaning of this Commandment, Jay Williams wrote:

> In effect the commandment says, if you use the name of God, be sure that you mean what you say. It is directed against the priest of Yahweh who lifts up God's name in order to further his own ambitions, against the elder who parades his religion in order to win friends and influence people, against the theologian who has become so accustomed to the name of God that it rolls off his tongue without thought or reverence.[5]

4. The Fourth Commandment calls upon God's covenant people to be good stewards of their time, maintaining a healthy balance between work

and worship. Seven days—not just one day—are included in the scope of this command: "Remember the sabbath day, to keep it holy. Six days you shall labor, and do all your work; but the seventh day is a sabbath to the Lord your God; in it you shall not do any work" (Ex. 20:8-10).

This Commandment calls for regularity and discipline in both work and worship. Many of us have overlooked the fact that the Decalogue contains a command to work. The constant witness of the Bible is to dignify honest toil and frown upon shiftless laziness. Work is not a vulgar task that the gentleman or lady should shun. It is, instead, a person's opportunity to join God in cooperative endeavor. God Himself is a working God. The apostle Paul coined the phrase, "If any one will not work, let him not eat" (2 Thess. 3:10). In keeping with this statement, every Jewish boy was taught some manual skill. Jesus was a carpenter; Paul, a tentmaker. This trait enhances rather than detracts from their statures as great religious teachers.

We are to work, but we are not to work all the time—so this Commandment would teach us. Our aggressive, competitive energy can make us work too hard, burning ourselves out and decreasing our efficiency. We can become "workaholics." We can depend too much on our own efforts, and forget God's overshadowing providence. As a rule, we will not forget to work, but we can easily forget to worship.

"Is it wrong for me to do this on Sunday?" is frequently heard today in reference to this Commandment. A specific book of rules cannot be given in answer to this question. This was the error of the Pharisees in Jesus' day. Generally speaking, anything that would be wrong on Sunday would also be wrong any other day of the week. As we have seen, this Commandment teaches that all of a person's time is a gift from God and should be held in careful stewardship.

Strange as it may seem, the great enemy of the sabbath today is excessive leisure. Leisure, or playtime, was not even mentioned in the Fourth Commandment. This is likely an indication that leisure is a luxury that is only known in modern times. We gladly affirm that the old proverb is true: "All work and no play makes Jack a dull boy." The current generation, however, needs to know that all play and no work or worship is equally devastating to mankind's good life on the earth.

The sin in breaking this Commandment is that we lose the multiple, balanced response for which it calls. Our times become out of joint. The increasing secularization of the Christian Sunday means that growing numbers of people treat Sunday as another day for business as usual. In our quest for greater profits, we may find ourselves morally and spiritually impoverished because we did not heed the wisdom of the Fourth Commandment.

I like what Page Kelley wrote about this Commandment:

> The meaning of the sabbath for Christians has been transferred from the seventh day to the first day of the week in celebration of the resurrection of Christ. What a blessed privilege to observe the Lord's Day! When we do so, all of life falls into the rhythmic pattern of meaningful work and festive rest. On this special day out of seven we lay down our strengths and our achievements at the feet of Him who created us for His praise and adoration. In a sense the sabbath expresses the essence of all the other Commandments, both in its religious as well as its social meaning.[6]

Respect for Persons

The first four Commandments have primary reference to our relationship with God. Reverence for God includes putting God first in our loyalties and priorities. That means refusing to allow any object, person, or idea to assume the role of "playing god" in our lives. It means that we take God's name in earnest, not in vain. It means that we acknowledge the importance and sanctity of time—organizing our days so that our lifestyles reflect a balance of work, rest (play), and worship.

The last six Commandments have primary concern with our relation to other people. A deep respect for others as persons made in the image of God underlies this part of the law of Moses. These Commandments provide basic guidelines for living in relation to one another. They speak to relationships within the home and society in general. Even the Commandments that are stated negatively are designed to promote and preserve such positive values as human life, marriage, property ownership, and personal reputation.

Some people say, "It's easy for me to love God. It's just other people that I can't stand!" Such a comment is most likely a subtle half-truth. It is really "not easy" to love God with all of our being. We are continually tempted to let some attitude or action fragment our wholehearted love for God. But most of us do have more trouble loving our neighbors than we do loving God. We can allow God to become distant and somewhat removed from our daily lives. But other people are always with us. Life is just one interpersonal relationship after another! And for most of us, this begins daily at home with our own families. That is exactly where the second table of the Decalogue begins.

5. The Fifth Commandment speaks directly to the strategic importance of stability and permanence in family relationships: "Honor your father and your mother, that your days may be long in the land which the Lord your God gives you" (Ex. 20:12).

Like the key role of the differential gear in an automobile, the home is the connecting link where the sphere of relating to God and the sphere of relating to one another most significantly meet. In the home and family, a child is first introduced to a world inhabited by other human beings. In like manner, the home is the cradle for first religious experiences. Here a child intuitively learns about the Heavenly Father, whom he cannot see or hear, through the visible presence and audible words of his earthly parents. In no other life experience does this meeting occur with such depth and significance. Probably more than most of us realize, there's no place like home!

The ideal for the home given by God to Moses is more concerned with people than with plans. Indeed, when the Ten Commandments were given at Sinai, the Israelites were still living in tents, moving gypsylike from Egypt to Canaan. An interest in well-constructed homes had not yet come. But the concern for depth and permanence in family relationships was keenly alive.

God commanded Moses to teach the people to honor their fathers and mothers (Ex. 20:12). "Fathers" are mentioned first in this Commandment. In a similar reference, "mothers" are mentioned first (Lev. 19:3). The rabbis usually quoted these two verses together, indicating that equal honor was to be given to both parents.

Paul observed that this was the first Commandment with promise (Eph. 6:2). By keeping this commandment, the Israelites were promised both *prosperity*—"that it may go well with thee" (Deut. 5:16, KJV), and *permanence*—"that thy days may be long upon the land which the Lord thy God giveth thee" (Ex. 20:12, KJV).

The practical wisdom in this Commandment should be apparent. Neither family nor nation can long achieve prosperity or permanence when family ties are not taken seriously. The family is the basic unit in every society. To strengthen the family is to strengthen the entire fabric of community and national life.

We should take careful note of the word "honor" in this Commandment. To honor is to respect, to regard with due obedience and courtesy. The family is the starting point for setting patterns of respect and obedience for mature judgment. A wholesome respect for proper authority is basic for the good and godly life.

The result of breaking this Commandment is miserable failure on the home front. Americans who are marrying seem to be enjoying it less. Divorce statistics are frighteningly high. Many couples live together without the formality and commitment of marriage. Some segments of the youth subculture are notoriously rebellious. Well-run, efficient nursing homes today provide needed and helpful service to many families with aging parents. However, some of these institutions are more like warehouses where the aging live and die, forgotten by family and friends.

6. The Sixth Commandment affirms the sacredness of human life: "You shall not kill" (Ex. 20:13). This command does not deify human life but does recognize that life is a gift from God. To destroy human life is to violate the image of God in human beings. "Whoever sheds the blood of man, by man shall his blood be shed; for God made man in his own image" (Gen. 9:6).

God gave this Commandment to protect the Israelites from one another. Respect for a neighbor's right to live is basic to good citizenship in an ordered society.

This Commandment did not, however, make Israel a pacifist nation, that is, a people who would not wage war. On a few occasions the people refused to fight on the sabbath, but mostly they were a warlike people who conquered Canaan by the sword and defended it zealously.

The Israelites also accepted the concept of capital punishment (Num. 15:32-36; 35:16-21). Punishment was given accordingly to a person's crime and could include death by stoning, burning, beheading, or strangling. In other words, it was never suggested that this Commandment forbade what we might call judicial killing.

The Jewish Law reflected the seriousness of sin, while showing mercy to the sinner. Elaborate precautions were observed to protect the rights of individuals, even the guilty. As an expression of this leniency, cities of refuge were established as havens for those who accidentally caused another person's death. The six cities of refuge were located so that no one would ever be far from one of them.

This Commandment against killing has probably had more success than any of the others in reaching its objective. Murder has become harder to pass off under a respectable name than any other sin involved in the Decalogue. Our heritage today contains centuries for growth in the respect for human life.

Nevertheless, the possibility for breaking this Commandment is real. The temptation to kill someone is probably the least of our worries. But what about driving safely? driving while intoxicated? the threat of nuclear holocaust? abortion on demand? the effects of smoking on smokers and nonsmokers? We need to let this Commandment prod us into a new awareness of the sacredness of human life.

7. The Seventh Commandment speaks directly to another area of vital concern: "You shall not commit adultery" (Ex. 20:14). This Commandment is actually related in both context and spirit to the Sixth and the Eighth Commandments. As we have just seen, the Sixth Commandment upholds a genuine respect for the sacredness of human personality. The Eighth Commandment, "You shall not steal," defends the right of ownership and respect for private property.

The Seventh Commandment includes both these concerns at the point of marriage. Adultery is debasing to all personalities involved. Those who truly respect the sacredness of human personhood should never violate it either by murder or adultery. Furthermore, according to the customs of ancient Judaism, the Jewish husband regarded his wife as a part of his property. Although in most homes the wife was the husband's most valued possession, she was still a possession. For an individual to commit adultery was to steal that for which he had no right.

The Seventh Commandment, in contrast to our sensate culture, declared adultery to be a major crime—in company with murder, theft, and perjury. The sin of adultery strikes at the heart of God's first institution for man and woman's welfare upon the earth—marriage and the home. The gravity of a sin can be somewhat judged by the penalty it receives. Jewish jurisprudence decreed death by stoning for the sin of adultery (see Lev. 20:10; John 8:1-11).

The wider scope of this Commandment affirms that there is nothing inherently wrong with our human sexuality. It is one of God's gifts to us (Gen. 1:27). Thus we may say that the Bible views sex as a tremendous and vital aspect of life. Sex can be known in covenant marriage as a source of great energy for good. This Commandment can help us discover the fullness and goodness of life.

The results of breaking this Commandment vary from organized prostitution to casual "affairs" within an office or neighborhood. Such high-risk sex shatters dreams, creates legitimate guilt, makes for disillusionment, and may contribute to fatal illnesses.

8. The Eighth Commandment declares simply and straightforwardly, "You shall not steal" (Ex. 20:15). Positively stated, this command upholds the right of private property. The law of Moses dignified this relationship between man and his possessions as a sacred covenant. Just as you have no right to take another man's life or his wife, you have no right to take his material wealth.

Property is gained in one of three ways: (1) by the free gift of another person, (2) by toil, or (3) by theft. The first two ways are based upon the necessary laws of human interrelationship: love and work. Theft violates both of these laws. The thief does not love the person from whom he steals, and he makes it difficult for the person sustaining a loss to love the thief. To steal violates the law of toil because the thief takes from another person that for which he did not work.

To take away a person's possessions by force or stealth hampers his ability to provide for himself and his family. Man has a moral right to own property. It represents his means of meeting personal and family needs. It also represents his independence from the control of other people by having material strength to resist.

Stealing is, thus, evil because ownership is good. Privately owned property is one of the basic orders of creation ordained by God for the welfare of the human race. To refrain from stealing is to respect God's purpose as well as the other person's individual right.

While the Bible defends the right to ownership, it also states that when we have and our neighbor has not our Christian duty is to share with our neighbor. If we do not, how can we callously brand as a thief the poor man who steals bread for his hungry children?

The sin of stealing can be both overt and direct, or subtle and devious. For example, the Eighth Commandment obviously prohibits embezzling and cheating on income tax. But does it also speak to "goofing off" at work, bribes and payoffs to increase sales, buying habits and prompt payment of bills? Some careful observers have said that almost all forms of economic dishonesty have reached epidemic levels in American society. Evidently many of us do not recognize the sin of breaking the Eighth Commandment.

9. The Ninth Commandment declares, "You shall not bear false witness against your neighbor" (Ex. 20:16). The command is concerned with mankind's power of speech and the fearful possibility of character assassination and personal destruction that it affords. Ordered society must be based upon a foundation of truth. Otherwise, all endeavor of mutual concern and interchange is hopelessly snarled.

The initial purpose of the Ninth Commandment was to uphold the sacredness of the judicial system—a foundation stone for any stable society. The verb in the command means "to answer," that is, in court, whether as plaintiff, defendant, or witness. It is not necessary, however, for a man to appear in court as a witness or an official in order to break this command. Its wider implications involve the more informal hazards of gossip, lying, and slander. The law of Moses recognized that all of life, not just the judgment of the courts, depends upon a straightforward commitment to the truth.

The sin of breaking this Commandment ranges from outright, illegal perjury to what we sometimes call "little white lies." Telling the truth is sometimes dangerous. We frequently say, "The truth hurts!" I have found two biblical phrases to be of help in stating a Christian standard for telling the truth.

The author of Ecclesiastes gave this good advice: "To every thing there is a season, and a time to every purpose under heaven: . . . a time to keep silence, and a time to speak" (3:1,7, KJV). At times, the truth must be shouted openly. At other times, it may be best that the truth be held in confidence.

Someone has suggested these three tests for the words we speak: (1) Are they true? (2) Are they kind? (3) Are they necessary? This homely, but wise, counsel was given by a grandfather to his grandchildren: "Always tell the truth, but don't always be tellin' it!"

Ephesians has an even better rule of thumb for truth telling. Paul urged those Christians to continue a steady pattern of growth toward Christian maturity by "speaking the truth in love" (4:15). These words well express a positive statement of the Ninth Commandment. The Christian, in addition to not bearing false witness against his neighbor, will earnestly attempt to speak the truth in love even when it costs him dearly.

10. The Tenth Commandment declares that at times, "wanting" is wrong: "You shall not covet your neighbor's house; you shall not covet your neighbor's wife, or his manservant, or his maidservant, or his ox, or his ass, or anything that is your neighbor's" (Ex. 20:17). The commandment against coveting is the most intensely personal standard in this section of the Decalogue because covetousness takes place in the quiet recesses of the human heart.

Coveting is the most subtle and deceitful of all sins. The word *covet* means to indulge in thoughts that tend to lead to the actions named in the precious Commandments. More specifically, as William Barclay wrote, "to covet is not merely to desire something which one does not possess; it is to desire something which one has no right to possess."[7]

The command against coveting is one of the early insights into the fact that the inner life of human beings determines their destiny. To foster grasping thoughts is to encourage grasping deeds. This Commandment's concern for motive rather than action is strikingly similar to the teaching of Jesus in the Sermon on the Mount. This Commandment brings the

Decalogue to the threshold of the New Testament understanding of morality.

The caution of this Commandment points to the danger of allowing desire to become selfish and inordinate. Such desire, like a fire burning out of control, can engulf a neighbor's property with little or no regard for the neighbor's right to be. Desire is a necessary quality of persons, but it must not be allowed to dominate people to the point that they lose control of themselves.

A person who breaks this Commandment uses all kinds of rationalizations: "I believe that I'm *worth* that. . . . If I *want* it, I *need* it. . . . Since I *need* it, I should *have* it. . . . In order to *have* it, I will do whatever is necessary to *get* it." This kind of thought pattern opens the door for immoral behavior: murder for hire or hire for murder, lie, cheat, steal, and kill in order to accomplish the deeply coveted goal.

Some of the worst forms of covetousness are directed toward intangible concerns. For example, some people passionately desire power and authority over others. Other people would do anything to gain social prominence and prestige. A recent generation of Americans was called "the status seekers." To some extent, each of us wants to be somebody. Too many persons, however, grab for status in any quick and easy way!

In laying bare the true nature of covetousness, the apostle Paul said bluntly that covetousness is idolatry (Eph. 5:5; Col. 3:5)! The Tenth Commandment in the last analysis brings us back to the First Commandment: "You shall have no other gods before me" (Ex. 20:3). Covetousness can allow some person, object, or idea other than God to become the all-consuming drive of our lives. To give anything that kind of allegiance to someone or something is idolatry.

We have reviewed "the Big Ten." Who can say, "I keep them all— every one of them"? No one. Paul was correct when he wrote, "For all have sinned, and come short of the glory of God" (Rom. 3:23, KJV).

"Sin" is to miss the mark by failing to measure up to these Commandments. "Iniquity" is trying to twist, or bend, these commands more to suit our own liking. It is the attempt to rewrite the script which God gave to Moses so that our own foibles of character are not as evident and painful. "Transgression" is openly rebelling against the truth and wisdom, which is reflected in the Decalogue, and seeking to live our lives as though there were no guidelines or boundaries except those which we determine for ourselves.

The period of the Judges in Israelite history—a time known as the dark ages in ancient Israel—is summarized by this epitaph: "In those days there was no king in Israel; every man did what was right in his own eyes" (Judg. 21:25). In other words, with no recognized transcendent authority, right and righteousness were subject to the whim and fancy of each individual. The end result of such anarchy was moral chaos. Do you see any parallel between the idea of "every man [doing] what was right in his own eyes," and contemporary exhortations like this: "Just feel free!" . . . "Let it all hang out!" . . . "Do your own thing!"?

In the aftermath of World War II, Elton Trueblood wrote of the Ten Commandments as being essential "foundations for reconstruction." Many of us think that they are still just that for today!

I have defined *sin* and examined the Ten Commandments. Now I want to consider some of the pictures of sin found in the teaching of Jesus.

The Description of Sin in the Sermon on the Mount

Both the Decalogue and the Sermon on the Mount are major revelations of God's intended will for the lives of His people on earth. Matthew introduced the Sermon on the Mount this way: "Seeing the crowds, he went up on the mountain, and when he sat down his disciples came to him. And he opened his mouth and taught them, saying" (Matt. 5:1-2). These words contain three implications that heighten the importance of what Jesus was about to say.

First, with a great crowd assembled, Jesus went up on the mountain, just as Moses had done. In Matthew's structure of his Gospel, the Sermon on the Mount is the New Torah for the kingdom of God. As the Decalogue was the heart of the Old Covenant, the Sermon on the Mount became the heart of the New Covenant.

Second, Jesus "sat down." In the religious services of that day, a Jewish teacher did not stand at a lectern or behind a pulpit in the synagogue to teach or preach. A Jewish rabbi sat down when he was going to speak officially. Our culture continues something of this tradition in college and university circles when we speak of an endowed chair of English or chemistry or philosophy. The professor who occupies that "chair position" is qualified to speak officially on the area of his particular academic discipline.

Jesus' sitting down indicated that He was going to make an official pronouncement on a given subject. With supreme grace and authority, He taught all who would hear how best to live!

Third, Matthew added that Jesus "opened his mouth." This meant far more than that He began speaking. This specific phrase in the Greek language was often used to indicate that a person of importance was going to say something of great significance, to speak an authoritative word of truth. As we might say today, this phrase meant that a person was going to "tell it like it is!"

The brief statement of Matthew 5:1-2 are like a trumpet fanfare declaring, "Now hear this!" Jesus was on the verge of making important pronouncements. The Sermon on the Mount was like the inaugural address of Jesus as the public figure. The old covenant which had been given through Moses was giving place to a new covenant which was coming through Jesus Christ. The old law which had been written on tablets of stone was to be fulfilled in a new law which would be written in the hearts of God's people (Jer. 31:31-34). The Sermon on the Mount is, indeed, a new law of love, intensifying rather than removing the requirement of the Ten Commandments.

By intensifying the claims of the Commandments, Jesus gave a new insight into what sin looks like. Sin would no longer be seen primarily as some kind of disobedience to the law or ceremonial uncleanliness. Sin would no longer be viewed primarily as an external act of known misbehavior. Jesus saw sin more in terms of inner thoughts than outer actions. He viewed sin primarily as being a broken love, not a broken law.

A characteristic statement in the Sermon on the Mount is: "'You have heard that it was said to the men of old. . . . But I say to you'" (Matt. 5:21-22). In several of these instances, Jesus quoted from the Ten Commandments. Rather than lessening the claim of the old law, He intensified it and made it more personal. Thus, as He Himself stated, Jesus came not to destroy the law, but to fulfill it (v. 17).

Jesus recognized His spiritual debt to the past. He knew that He was not entering a religious vacuum in first-century Palestine. Neither was He a religious revolutionary in the sense that He would do away with everything that had preceded Him. He closely identified Himself with the law, the prophets, and the psalms of His people.

Jesus gave serious place to the law in His religious priorities (Matt. 5:17-18). The new freedom He gave was never thought to be a moral license. His disciples were instructed to know the law and teach it to fellow believers. Jesus differed from the scribes and Pharisees, however, in His interpretation of the law. He exalted the moral and spiritual dimensions of the law. He did not regard the ritual and ceremonial requirements as of central importance.

In the mind of Christ, a person's righteousness was not just a cold matter of legal obedience. Instead, it was a living relationship with the God who gave the law. In this way, Jesus fulfilled the purpose of the Old Testament law. He also brought the complete revelation of the Lord who had first revealed Himself to Moses at the burning bush. In other words, Jesus preserved the root of the old law given by God at Sinai, but He pointed to new insights for His followers. Like the scribe who had been made a disciple of the kingdom of heaven, Jesus brought "out of his treasure things new and old" (Matt. 13:52, KJV).

In regard to the law, Jesus taught neither a new legalism nor lawlessness. He always took the Scripture seriously, but He did not make the letter of the law supreme. To those who wanted to cast aside the law— even to relaxing "one of the least of these commandments" (v. 19)— Jesus voiced His strong opposition. He would not tolerate moral license in the name of Christian liberty. He called for a righteousness that would exceed that of the scribes and Pharisees (v. 20).

Frank Stagg concluded: "Jesus accepted the Old Testament law in principle and as permanently binding, but he interpreted Scripture by Scripture, elevating the moral and ethical demands and the primacy of the personal above ritual laws. To him, what ultimately mattered were God and man—not sabbath, purification of hands, and the like."[8]

In light of this, we should not be surprised to see that in the Sermon on the Mount Jesus made specific reference to some of the Commandments.

Rather than forbidding murder and killing, Jesus tackled the problem of unresolved anger—especially unfounded hostility (Matt. 5:21-22). Rather than dealing with adultery and other acts of sexual immorality, Jesus emphasized the need for self-control to defuse all lust (vv. 27-31). Rather than calling upon His followers to tell the truth just when they were testifying in court, Jesus said that citizens in the kingdom of heaven would tell the truth at *all* times and places. No oath would be necessary for their yes to mean yes and their no to mean no (vv. 33-37)!

Jesus reversed the Jewish understanding of the lex talionis, the law of retaliation. That code required revenge to be sought—"An eye for an eye and a tooth for a tooth" (v. 38; see also Ex. 21:24). Jesus said that His followers would not seek such revenge. Instead, they would respond with turning the other cheek, going the second mile, giving cloak as well as coat (vv. 38-41).

In a similar vein, rather than demonstrating a simplistic life-style in which friends were loved and enemies hated, Jesus taught that citizens of the kingdom of heaven were to march to the beat of a different drummer. They were to love their enemies, as well as their friends (vv. 43-48). Thus, Jesus presented the picture of sin as being an act or attitude which violates the law of love.

Although not a part of the Sermon on the Mount, a later incident in Jesus' life illustrates this point. During the final week of His ministry in Jerusalem, the Pharisees and Sadducees were trying to trap Jesus in His speech. Matthew reported that one of them asked Jesus a question about the Commandments (22:34-40). The questioner was a lawyer among the Pharisees, a person, no doubt, of much training. He asked his question "to test" (v. 35) Jesus: "Teacher, which is the great commandment in the law?" (v. 36).

Jesus' answer was actually a dual command. He defined the "great" command as entailing man's duty to love God with all that he is and has (v. 37). "This," Jesus said, "is the *great* and *first* commandment" (v. 38, author's italics). Then He significantly added, "And a second is like it, You shall love your neighbor as yourself. On these two commandments depend all the law and the prophets" (vv. 39-40).

These commands would have been familiar to His Jewish hearers. The

first came directly from the Shema (Deut. 6:4-5), a well-known call to
worship in synagogue and Temple services. The second command was
found in Leviticus 19:18. Thus, Jesus made use of the noble religious
heritage of the Jews.

Jesus' summary of the law is a reflection in miniature of the Ten Commandments. The dual command to love God and one's neighbor expresses the essence of the two tables in the Decalogue. Both the tables of
the law and the commands of Jesus are bound inseparably together. Either of the two alone gives a distorted emphasis.

Thus We Conclude

Sin is our failure to keep the Ten Commandments. These commands
teach us how to have a proper reverence for God and respect for our
fellowman. They are not expressions of God's arbitrary will and His
despotic nature. They are rather authentic guidelines, set forth by the
great Creator God, which will help us discover the secret of how life can
best be lived.

Sin is even more our failure to love—to love God first and then to love
our neighbors as we love ourselves. Our sin is sometimes couched in the
subtle temptation to separate these great loves—to suppose that we can
sincerely love God and be oblivious to the needs of other people or that
we can be compassionately humanitarian in helping other people with no
thought of our relationship to God.

Sin can also come from our failure to deal with both the actual deed
and the underlying motive behind any single sinful act. Jesus taught His
followers to monitor carefully both their deeds and their thoughts. He
wanted the *fruit* of sin in life to be removed, but he also wanted the *roots*
of sin in the human heart to be changed. Long before the emphasis of
much current psychological thought, Jesus recognized the importance of
inner attitudes determining outer behavior patterns. "For out of the
abundance of the heart," Jesus said, "the mouth speaks" (Matt. 12:34;
see also vv. 33-35).

With the emphasis upon self-affirmation in much popular thought today, we need to realize that Jesus' summary of the law included a third
level of love: "You . . . shall love yourself." Selfishness, or ignoble self-

love, is strongly akin to covetousness. Never can this find an appropriate place in the Christian's heart. But Christians should maintain a basic self-respect. We should acknowledge the rights and privileges of our neighbors, looking upon them as individuals created in the image of God. We should grant ourselves a similar respectability. Each of these two, or "three," loves is best experienced when all are held in dynamic relationship to the other.

Notes

1. Roy L. Honeycutt, "Exodus," Revised, *The Broadman Bible Commentary* (Nashville: Broadman Press, 1973) 1:389.

2. William Barclay, *The Ten Commandments for Today* (New York: Harper & Row, 1973), p. 14.

3. Ibid., p. 12.

4. Joy Davidman, *Smoke on the Mountain* (Philadelphia: The Westminster Press, 1958), p. 16.

5. Jay G. Williams, *Ten Words of Freedom* (Philadelphia: Fortress Press, 1971), p. 137.

6. Page H. Kelley, *Exodus: Called for Redemptive Mission* (Nashville: Convention Press, 1977), p. 116.

7. William Barclay, *The Ten Commandments for Today* (New York: Harper & Row Publishers Inc., 1973), p. 196.

8. Frank Stagg, "Matthew," *The Broadman Bible Commentary* (Nashville: Broadman Press, 1969) 8:108.

5

Can We Cite Specific Sins and Sinners from the Bible?

The primary message of the Bible is to make known the good news of God's salvation which is offered to all people through Jesus Christ. The Bible is thus salvation history, focusing on the activity of God from the time of creation to the time of consummation. Therefore, it follows that the Bible message is primarily concerned with the "good news" of what God has done to redeem mankind by faith, not the "bad news" about the sinfulness of man.

The Bible does, however, take sin seriously—very seriously. The salvation history of the Bible is the story of God's revelation of Himself to redeem mankind from sin and to restore fellowship with human beings which has been broken by sin. Consequently, the Bible has much to say about what may be called the down-to-earth, nitty-gritty aspects of human sin.

The Bible declares that sin is missing the mark of what God intended for His people. Sin is an exercise in human freedom whereby we may twist, or distort, the purpose of God. Sin is the result of forthright human disobedience and outright human rebellion against the clearly revealed will of God. This chapter will show how these definitions of sin have been "fleshed out" in real life, as reported in some of the incidents in biblical history.

Specific Sins and Sinners in the Old Testament

The Sin of Idolatry (Ex. 32—34)

A sense of drama surrounded the Israelites as Moses went up Mount Sinai to meet the Lord and receive the law. Moses had involved all of the people in the special preparations for this event of utmost importance (Ex. 19:9-15). The people had readily accepted their responsibility in the covenant agreement which the Lord was offering to them. When they heard the proposal from Moses and the elders, the people made a vow of consecration and commitment: "All that the Lord has spoken, we will do" (v. 8).

But Moses was delayed in coming down from Mount Sinai (Ex. 32:1), and the people too quickly gave up on his return. They unwisely took matters into their own hands, went to Aaron, Moses' brother, and demanded. "Up, make us gods who shall go before us; as for Moses, the man who brought us up out of the land of Egypt, we do not know what has become of him" (v. 1).

In response to this plea, Aaron directed the people to pool their earrings of gold. These were made into a molten mass, and with an engraving tool, Aaron fashioned a golden calf (v. 4). The diminutive term "calf" probably does not convey the full impact of this graven image. The word *bull* would more likely give us the picture. Concerning this designation, Roy Honeycutt commented, "The fashioning of a golden calf reflects the almost universal equation of the bull with vigor and strength in the Ancient Near East."[1]

The crass irony of Israel's sin could hardly be more vividly drawn. Moses was atop Mount Sinai receiving the crucial Ten Words in awesome encounter with the Living God, while God's impatient people were at the foot of the same mountain preparing to worship a man made bull!

But attempting to replace the Creator with a molten creature was just the beginning of sin for the people. Aaron built an altar before the golden bull. He proclaimed that the next day would be a time of feasting and celebration. The following day the people made offerings to their idol (v. 6).

The Exodus narrative also reports that "the people sat down to eat and drink and rose up to play" (v. 6). Honeycutt said, "The verb translated *to play* suggests sexual orgies which accompanied fertility rites, especially in Canaanite Baalism."[2] An Archie Bunker might aptly say, "Put a bull in God's place, and what do you expect!"

Clearly idolatry does not long remain just a simple matter of who or what is taking over the role of God. When we tamper with God, we quickly tamper with the whole of life. To be sure, people are far more than mindless dominoes. But topping God in the lead position does far more than just replace a deity. It starts a chain reaction which can affect all of life and morals. It was that way at Sinai, and it is still the same today.

The Sin of Covetousness and Disobedience
(Josh. 8; 1 Sam. 15)

Failure to follow God's directions, especially when they are made explicitly clear, results in sin. Such sin can be both personal and social in its implications and its consequent judgment.

Joshua had succeeded Moses as the leader of the people. After the long delay of wandering in the wilderness for forty years, the people had finally crossed the Jordan River into Canaan. Jericho, the ancient fortress city in the Jordan Valley, had fallen into the hands of the Israelites. By the custom of that day, most of the booty in Jericho was named as "devoted things"—that is, they were to be totally destroyed as an act of sacrifice and worship to Yahweh (God) who had brought the Israelites victory in battle.

Joshua had made this word from God quite clear to the people on the eve of victory: "But you, keep yourselves from the things devoted to destruction, lest when you have devoted them you take any of the devoted things and make the camp of Israel a thing for destruction, and bring trouble upon it. But all the silver and gold, and vessels of bronze and iron, are sacred to the Lord; they shall go into the treasury of the Lord" (Josh. 6:18-19).

The walls of Jericho did come tumbling down. Joshua and the people had a complete victory. Yet unknown to Joshua at the time, some of the people of Israel broke faith in regard to the "devoted things" in Jericho (7:1). More specifically, a man by the name of Achan from the tribe of Judah secretly took some of these things. He later learned that the sin of coveting and outright disobedience against God's expressed will is not easily hidden.

Achan's sin became known in this way. Israel's next military engagement was against Ai, a fortress position which would give the invaders a foothold in the hill country overlooking the Jordan Valley. Since Ai was smaller than Jericho, Joshua dispatched an assault force of about three thousand men (v. 4), rather than the entire army, evidently thinking it would be an easy victory for Israel.

The Israelite force was routed with a loss of some thirty-six casualties (v. 5). The military loss was not devastating in itself, but the psychological loss was, as W. H. Morton observed, "of panic proportions."[3] For the Israelites, the defeat brought the fear that God was no longer with them. With agonizing mourning rites, Joshua and the elders sought the counsel of God for the reason for the defeat (vv. 6-9). God's answer was forthright: "Israel has sinned; they have transgressed my covenant which I commanded them; they have taken some of the devoted things; they have stolen, lied, and put them among their own stuff" (v. 11).

In essence, God told Joshua that the root of sin in Israel had to be found and uprooted. In a ceremony which likely involved the casting of sacred lots (v. 14; see also 1 Sam. 10:2-24), the tribe of Judah was isolated, then the family and the household of Achan. Finally, the lot fell on Achan himself, and he admitted his guilt. He told of seeing certain beautiful things among the spoils at Jericho: "I coveted them, and took them" (v. 21).

Retribution against Achan was swift. Little was known at this point in Israel's life about the doctrine of forgiveness. Achan was not even forgiven one time, much less "seventy times seven" (Matt. 18:22). Achan and all of his family and his possessions were stoned and burned. So did the Israelites remove sin from their midst. W. H. Morton wrote that this story "is a classic illustration of the ancient social concept of community solidarity. In such a society, the whole group was held guilty for the sin of one of its members, whose punishment then devolved upon the members of his immediate family."[4]

Although we no longer think of sin and guilt with such family-block graphics, we kid ourselves if we think that individual sin affects only the person, or persons, directly involved. Families, and many other people, still pay the price for an individual's sin. Fortunately, for us, the price is not usually death. But still, somebody always has to help pay the price for our sins.

You may think that Achan was so ruthlessly treated because he was just an ordinary foot soldier. If he had had more rank, he might have fared better. A later Old Testament incident indicates that such would not necessarily have been the case.

At the instruction of the Lord, Samuel, the last of the great judges in Israel, had anointed Saul to become the first king of God's people (1 Sam. 10:1-2). Saul had many physical gifts which seem to equip him well for that office. Saul's moral character, however, was weak and caused his downfall.

Through the Lord and Samuel, Saul was instructed to destroy completely a longtime enemy of the Israelites—the Amalekites and their leader, King Agag (15:1-3). They were to spare, or save, nothing. As in the case of Achan, God's directive was clear.

But Saul did not heed God. He took King Agag captive, and he spared the best of the livestock of the Amalekites. Later when Samuel approached the king, Saul lied, reporting that he had done what the Lord commanded (v. 13). With a kind of Catch 22 question, Samuel knowingly asked Saul, "What then is this bleating of the sheep in my ears, and the lowing of the oxen" (v. 14)?

Saul again lied, as he replied, "The people spared the best of the sheep and of the oxen, to sacrifice to the Lord your God" (v. 15). Actually, there was no earlier indication that this was what Saul and his soldiers planned to do. Samuel could well have said in disgust, "Likely story!"

Samuel's actual reply to Saul should be preserved in bold-faced type. They were initially spoken to Saul, but they at times need to be heard by all of us. Samuel said,

> "Has the Lord as great delight in burnt offerings
>   and sacrifices,
>   as in obeying the voice of the Lord?
> Behold, to obey is better than sacrifice,
>   and to hearken than the fat of rams,
> For rebellion is as the sin of divination,
>   and stubborness is as iniquity and idolatry"
>   (vv. 22-23).

Samuel's concluding words to Saul on that occasion had an awesome finality about them: "Because you have rejected the word of the Lord, he has also rejected you from being king" (v. 23). In Samuel's understanding of life, not even the king could expect to live as though he were above God's will and righteousness.

So, whether a foot soldier, Achan, or a king, Saul, covetousness and disobedience to God's expressed will were considered quite serious offenses. They once caused a soldier and his family to lose their lives and a king to lose his crown.

The Sin of Wanton Sexual Assault and Violence (Judg. 19—21)

The period of the judges in ancient Israel is known as the dark ages in Israelite history. The last three chapters in the Book of Judges comprise a section which is sometimes considered an appendix to the book. The series of incidents recorded in these chapters, which are sometimes called the outrage at Gibeah, certainly point up the moral degradation of the time. It is a sordid story of gang rape, violence, and vendetta.

Briefly, this is the account given. A certain Levite who lived in the hill country of Ephraim north of Jerusalem (Judg. 19:1), had married a concubine from Bethlehem in Judah, south of Jerusalem. In time, some kind of problem arose in the marriage. The concubine became very angry with the Levite and went home to her father (v. 2).

Some four months later the Levite went to Bethlehem to attempt a reconciliation with his estranged wife (v. 2b). His father-in-law was overjoyed to see him. On the fifth day, after celebrating the renewal of family ties, the Levite decided to return home. He and his wife and a servant began the journey late in the afternoon. They thought of staying overnight in the city of the Jebusites (Jerusalem), but then travelled farther to the town of Gibeah.

At Gibeah, the three people waited in the town square, as was the custom, hoping someone would show hospitality to them as strangers. An old man, returning from work in his field (v. 16), invited them to his house (v. 20).

They went to the old man's house, cared for their animals, washed their feet, and sat down together for an evening meal (v. 21). This relaxed atmosphere was rudely interrupted as the house was surrounded by some "base fellows" from the town (v. 22). The men beat on the door, demanding that the old man bring his male guest outside to them. They intended to use him for their own homosexual desire (v. 22).

The old man refused to release his male guest under such circumstances. However, he offered his own virgin daughter and the Levite's concubine to satisfy the lust of the men of Gibeah (v. 24). But the men of Gibeah would not accept the substitutes. In an impulsive act of almost unbelievable selfishness, the Levite shoved his concubine out the door to the aroused mob of men. The narrative gives this sordid report: " . . . they knew her, and abused her all night until the morning. And as the dawn began to break, they let her go" (v. 25). The poor woman, certainly in a state of shock, struggled back to the old man's home and fell at the threshold of the door. Shortly thereafter, when the Levite came out to resume his journey, he found his concubine dead!

The Levite took the body of his concubine home to Ephraim. There he "took a knife, and . . . divided her, limb by limb, into twelve pieces" (v. 29). He sent these grim reminders of sexual assault and violence throughout the land (20:1). He wanted the entire nation to know of the horrible thing that had occurred at Gibeah, a town in that part of the land which was assigned to the tribe of Benjamin.

A strong spirit of national indignation arose against Gibeah and the Benjaminites, that such a sin could occur among the people of God. A combined Israelite army was mustered to destroy Gibeah. The Benjaminites rallied to defend it. The first two Israelite attacks against Gibeah and the Benjaminites were not successful. The sons of Benjamin were fierce fighters. The third assault against Gibeah, however, was successful. The town was totally destroyed, and over 25,000 Benjaminites were slain (v. 46).

The continuing national anguish over the outrage of Gibeah for a time appeared to threaten the continued existence of the tribe of Benjamin. After their military victory, the men of Israel had taken an oath at Mizpah not to intermarry with the Benjaminites (21:1). In time, however, this sentiment relented to the point that the people did not want the tribe of Benjamin blotted out of the nation. Provision was made to allow non-Israelite women to marry Benjaminites. Thus the tribe was preserved.

What can this crude, shocking account of rape and violence say to us today? In the first place, it is still possible for human sexuality to become so base and degenerate that its expression is crude and shocking. Once in my pastoral ministry, I was made aware of a Saturday night "beer bust" for a group of men at a local motel which degenerated to the point that it assumed some striking parallels to the outrage at Gibeah. We are not correct when we say or think that nothing like this goes on today.

Secondly, when standards of morality reach their lowest common denominator, man's capacity for inhumanity to other persons knows almost no bounds. From the days of Noah, to the time of Aaron and the golden bull, to the outrage at Gibeah—human moral behavior sometimes seems more akin to animals than to people made in the image of God.

In the third place, when the moral code is determined by every person doing what is right in his own eyes, moral chaos and anarchy result. An ordered society must have a relationship with God whereby standards of right and wrong conduct may be nurtured and maintained.

The Sin of Moral Corruption on a National Scale (Isa. 5)

Midway through the eighth century BC, Isaiah, the great statesman-prophet of Jerusalem, found himself living in a generation that seemed hopelessly confused in its moral and spiritual values. With compassionate earnestness, Isaiah dissected his society, seeking to reveal the lurking danger of a decadent morality. The oracle, or sermon, recorded in Isaiah 5 indicates his forthrightness and inspiration as a prophet.

The occasion was likely one of the great gatherings in the Temple during the Feast of Tabernacles, the harvest festival in Judah. Isaiah had a serious message for the holiday-spirited crowd. With versatility and cleverness he chose an unusual approach to the unpleasant subject of sin.

As the familiar vintage songs were being sung, Isaiah adopted the role of a ballad singer and introduced a new song (5:1-2). The crowd gathered to hear the familiar court prophet as he sang in the informal setting.

The ballad was the story of a vineyard (vv. 1-2). In good folk-singer style, Isaiah told how the owner had carefully chosen the vineyard "on a very fertile hill." He carefully prepared the soil and planted choice vines. He protected the vineyard and made preparations for a good yield.

Rather than producing good grapes, however, the vines grew "wild grapes" (v. 4), or stink berries. In disgust, the owner tore down the wall and left the vineyard exposed to the ravages of nature (vv. 5-6).

Having gained the rapt attention of the crowd, Isaiah was ready to make his point (v. 7). The vineyard in the song was the nation of Judah, and God was the devoted owner. God was disgusted with the nation. Having been given every providential opportunity, the people failed to produce what God desired. In a clever play on words, which is evident only in the Hebrew, Isaiah said that God had expected justice *(mishpat),* but found instead bloodshed *(mispah)*. God had wanted to find righteousness *(tsedaqah)* reigning among the people, but discovered only the sorrowful cry *(tseaqah)* of the oppressed. Judah had no alternative but to expect God's judgment. Rather than concluding with a hopeful refrain, Isaiah's dolefully sad ballad ended with details of the sins of the people which were bringing shame and destruction upon the nation. His moral analysis of his century has a frightening contemporary ring.

In a series of six "woes," Isaiah laid bare the sickness of the society. The first woe decried the land-grabbing tendencies of Jewish farmers (vv. 8-10). The democratic agrarian ideal for Judah, whereby every man would "sit under his vine and under his fig tree" (Mic. 4:4), was being lost. With the inflationary times, the small landowner was disappearing, and some estates grew larger and larger. The displaced families tended to become serfs in a feudal-type society. Isaiah saw that moral deterioration would follow in the wake of this basic shift in the social structure. He predicted loneliness for the landowners, as they were increasingly isolated in the solitude of their wealth (vv. 8*b*-9), and barrenness for the land (v. 10).

Two of the woes, the second and the sixth, lamented the evil of strong drink in Jewish society. In a prosperous culture grown fat with luxury, the feast of the social and political leaders were becoming drunken revels. Partying began early and lasted late (v. 11). With sharp satire, Isaiah ridiculed the men who became the heroes and valiant ones of the drinking tables under the deceitful influence of wine (v. 22).

Isaiah described the result of excessive drinking as spiritual atrophy (v. 12). The people had an era for popular music from the "lyre and harp, timbrel and flute," but they were deaf to the deeds of the Lord.

They saw that the best wines were at their feasts, but they were blind to the work of God's hands.

In the third woe, Isaiah used a graphic metaphor from rural life to picture the status of men who obstinately choose to remain in sin. Isaiah felt that many of his peers had become unconsciously harnessed to sin (v. 18), so that it followed them about "as easily as the unresisting farm beast on the end of a rope."⁵ Such men became flippant skeptics, doubting that God made Himself known in this world (v. 19).

The fourth woe stated by Isaiah was perhaps the most devastating of all. Many people in his society had utterly confused moral values. Due to ignorance and the progressive drag of sin, their ethical taste distinctions were dulled. As Isaiah expressed it, they could not distinguish between good and evil, light and darkness, sweet and bitter (v. 20).

Oblivious to their pitiful confusion, however, the people grew proud and conceited in their estimation of themselves. Basking in the affluent luxury of their day, the people regarded themselves as clever, shrewd operators, indeed!

In the fifth woe, Isaiah pointed to the folly of such conceited pride (v. 21). Sorrowfully, he looked upon his people as wise fools who, though they thought they knew much, understood little. Isaiah's words are like an overture to the later New Testament counsel, "Let any one who thinks that he stands take heed lest he fall" (1 Cor. 10:12).

As indicated, the sixth, or last, woe pointed to the dangerous role of strong drink in society. Isaiah made direct correlation between alcohol consumption and moral corruption (vv. 22-23). In the general decline of that day, it was probably inevitable that the courts would become involved. With consciences dulled by both a poor sense of value and excessive drinking, the judicial officials succumbed to bribery and maljudgment (v. 23).

Isaiah realistically saw little hope for improvement in the moral climate of his country. The momentum of the people on the toboggan slide of sin was increasing rather than diminishing. Consequently, because of their outright rejection of God's way, they could only expect retribution and judgment. Isaiah pictured the doom to follow as the burning of chaff and the withering of plants (v. 24).

Later history vindicated Isaiah in his severe warning. During his ministry in Jerusalem, the Northern Kingdom of Israel fell to Assyria in 722 BC, never to rise again. Judah progressively deteriorated, finally falling to the Babylonians around 586 BC.

We sometimes ponder the possibility that history may repeat itself. Isaiah's moral analysis and evaluation of his generation should make us shudder as we think of the social evils of our day. Striking parallels make the two eras very similar.

For example, note the farm situation. The past two decades have seen an acceleration in the basic shift in our agriculture population which has actually been going on for some time. Due to increased mechanization and cost of operation, farming is now big business. In many instances, the small farmer has had to sell out or declare bankruptcy.

In our generation, this has been a matter of economic necessity more than pressure from a scheming land-hungry aristocracy. But the social consequences are largely the same. Landless people tend to create unemployment problems in farming communities, or they huddle together in ghettos in the larger cities, areas where delinquency and crime are high. Agricultural experts are saying that the plight of the American farmer is the worst it has been since the Great Depression in the 1930s.

Consider the growing rate of alcohol consumption in the United States. This nation has become one of the "wettest" nations in the modern world, second only to France in the per capita use of beverage alcohol. Since 1940 the drinking population and the number of confirmed alcoholics have both skyrocketed. Any of the liquor statistics are staggering, but the most alarming are those reporting high school and college drinking. Since the repeal of Prohibition, the liquor industry has persistently tried to make youth and young adults liquor conscious. Tragically, they have succeeded. The most dangerous drinking age for adolescents is reported to be fourteen.

Add to this our confused sense of moral values, our smug intellectual pride, our unconscious attachments to the petty sins and prejudices of our culture, our growing awareness of grave moral lapses in the judiciary and Isaiah's eighth-century BC folksong to the Jews seems to be a report on how the young and the old in America live today! Because of our sin, we too may be judged!

Specific Sins and Sinners in the New Testament

Specific sins and sinners are also clearly delineated in the New Testament. The coming of Jesus into the world was heralded as being "good news of a great joy . . . to all the people" (Luke 2:10). This good news message declared that God in Christ is life and light and love (John 1:1-4; 3:16; 1 John 4:8-12). In spite of such gloriously positive affirmation, however, sin remained a persistent, nagging problem for mankind in general, and for the new Christian churches in particular.

The Sin of Hypocrisy and Lying (Acts 5)

In telling the story of life in the early church, Luke reported both moments of achievement and times of dissension. The same narrative which tells us of the Day of Pentecost (2:1-47) and the conversion of Saul of Tarsus (9:1-22) reports divisive murmuring in the Jerusalem congregation over the treatment of widows (6:1-7) and sharp disagreement over the acceptance of Gentile believers (15:1-11). Luke did not idealize the era and the people about whom he wrote. He told it like it really was!

Such historical realism is seen clearly in the deceitful actions of a married couple, Ananias and Sapphira, in the Jerusalem congregation (5:1-11). The entire Jerusalem congregation had been impressed with the generous spirit of Barnabas (4:36), who had sold a field which belonged to him and given the money to the disciples for church-related charities (v. 37). Ananias and his wife observed the acclaim which Barnabas received and were envious of his honor.

With Sapphira's consent, Ananias sold a piece of property (5:1-2), following the example of Barnabas. Unlike Barnabas, however, Ananias did not give the congregation all of the money from the sale of the property. Ananias voluntarily decided to sell his land. With no external pressure, he gave some of his newly acquired cash to the apostles for the ministry of the church. The sin of Ananias and Sapphira was not that they "kept back some of the proceeds" of the sale (v. 2) but that they wanted it to look like they had given all.

When Ananias brought his deceitful gift to the apostles, Peter saw through the farce. He pointed out that Ananias was not only lying to his fellow church members but was also lying "to the Holy Spirit" (v. 3) and "to God" (v. 4). Such willful deceit was a grievous blunder. Frank Stagg wrote:

> In the New Testament no sin is considered more serious than that of willful blindness to or rejection of the truth. Those who crucified Jesus did so with eyes deliberately closed to truth and right, and it is in connection with this disposition that the unpardonable sin is declared. Some defense may be made for sins of ignorance or weakness, but none can be made for willful blindness to truth or willful rejection of light. If the consequences to Ananias and Sapphira seem unduly severe, it must be recognized that the view taken here toward dishonesty at the foundation of one's character is no more serious than that reflected in the Gospels. Sin against the Holy Spirit—deliberate rejection of truth and right—is inexcusable. The sinner, if he turns from it, may be forgiven, but the sin itself is inexcusable.[6]

When Ananias realized that Peter clearly read his deceit and diagnosed his lie, he was overwhelmed. The shock was so devastating that Ananias "fell down and died" (v. 5). Concerning this abrupt demise, T. C. Smith wrote: "Probably his death came as a result of an awareness that he was exposed. In ancient times when a person knowingly violated a taboo, the shock was so great that sometimes it brought death. Uzzah put his hand on the ark of the covenant to steady it and died (2 Sam. 6:6f)."[7]

Three hours later, Sapphira came in, "not knowing what had happened" (v. 7). Peter quizzed her about the sale of the land, and she repeated the same lie as Ananias. Peter then exposed her deceit and reminded her that her sin also was against the Spirit of the Lord (v. 9). He also informed her of her husband's death. Again the shock was devastating. Sapphira fell down and died.

These sudden double deaths create a serious moral dilemma. Did Peter cause these deaths, or were they arbitrary acts from God Himself? Frank Stagg offered this conclusion to the matter·

> The prevailing New Testament view seems to be that wrath is operative as a natural, not arbitrary law; sin is serious enough to carry its own consequences. Many have concluded that Ananias and Sapphira died of shock, not by the arbitrary decree of God. This view, if true, is more readily harmonized with the larger New Testament teaching. These deaths can be

accounted for psychologically. The many signs accomplished in those days gave all the believers an awareness of divine power operative in their midst and struck awe and fear in their hearts. The sudden exposure of Ananias' sin against God could easily have produced the shock resulting in his death. Sapphira experienced that shock and also the shock that came with the news of her husband's death.[8]

Today news media occasionally report situations in which an individual being investigated for charges of embezzlement and fraud unexpectedly experienced a massive coronary and died. From the first century or from our era, such terminal occurrences have happened.

The Sin of Immorality (Luke 18:9-17; 1 Cor. 5:1-13)

Drawing a line to distinguish moral behavior from immoral behavior is never an easy thing to do. The Pharisees in Jesus' day marked off the perimeters of righteous living and then prided themselves in their own self-defined righteousness. The Pharisees looked with vain disdain upon people who did not measure up to their preconceived notions of morality.

One of the well-known parables of Jesus illustrates well this dimension of Pharisaical pride and self-righteousness (Luke 18:9-17). A Pharisee and a publican went up to the Temple to pray. The Pharisee thanked God that he was not a sinner like most other men. He practiced fasting, and he was a good tither (vv. 11-12). In contrast to such preening, the publican humbly asked for God's mercy (v. 13).

Jesus concluded His parable by saying that the publican, not the Pharisee, went home justified—that is, forgiven and made right with God. Jesus said, "For every one who exalts himself will be humbled, but he who humbles himself will be exalted" (v. 14).

The subtle nature of the Pharisee's pride may be illustrated by this incident which could have happened in any church. A faithful Sunday School teacher had taught this parable to her class with careful detail. She concluded the lesson by saying, "Now let us close with prayer, thanking God *that we are not like that Pharisee!*"

In spite of this possible moral sandtrap, we are called upon at times to say a clear yes or no to what is right or wrong. In his day, Paul urged the

Christians in Corinth to make that kind of decision concerning a wayward fellow church member.

A man, who was a member of the congregation, was "living with his father's wife" (1 Cor. 5:1). The woman involved was evidently the man's stepmother, not his own mother. It is not clear whether his father were dead or whether he had divorced the woman. The man and woman were living together sexually without being married to one another. This illicit relationship was common knowledge among members of the church.

Paul forthrightly declared that the divorce of religion and ethics, which this kind of relationship implied, was totally intolerable. The Corinthian believers had somehow allowed their moral judgment to become dull in dealing with this particular affair.

Corinth in the first century was a notoriously immoral site. Listed as one of the big four cities of the Mediterranean world—along with Rome, Alexandria, and Ephesus—Corinth was a center for commerce, transportation, and the arts. It was also a focal point for pagan worship, with the temple of Aphrodite located on the Acrocorinth—the high place of the city—overlooking the Bay of Corinth and the entire urban area. According to historians of that era, at one time this temple was served by a thousand sacred prostitutes. Because of lax morals and pagan religious rites, "to Corinthianize" was a proverbial expression for immoral behavior.[9] Against such a backdrop, Paul called upon Christians in Corinth to demonstrate a morally superior life-style.

In the same letter that urged that this Christian brother and fellow church member be properly disciplined, Paul listed ten kinds of immoral behavior which were not compatible with a Christian life-style. Raymond Brown designated this list as "a solemn roll call of the disinherited."[10] Paul named these sinners as follows: the immoral, idolaters, adulterers, homosexuals, thieves, greedy, drunkards, revilers, and robbers (6:9-10). People who practice such unrighteousness, Paul said, "will not inherit the kingdom of God" (v. 9). To keep the moral boundaries between life in the world and life in the church from becoming hopelessly blurred, some kind of discipline was needed in Corinth. It is likely needed in our churches today. Such discipline is best administered personally rather than institutionally. Christian discipline also endeavors to be more redemptive than punitive.

The Sin of Personal Disagreements Which Bring Rifts in Friendship and Ministry (Acts 13:1-5, 13-14; 15:36-41)

Not all sin reported in the New Testament was dramatic. Good people can disagree until their strong viewpoints result in divisive alienation and personal hurt. Such alienation is the fruit of sin, however open and innocent the circumstances may be that cause them. Fine Christian people at times do err and wound one another grievously. Like "white-collar" theft, such misbehavior may appear polite and genteel, but it is still sin. An episode in the relationship of Paul and Barnabas and John Mark illustrates this.

Under God's leadership, the church in Antioch of Syria decided to send out Barnabas and Paul as missionaries. Mark, a cousin of Joseph Barnabas (Col. 4:10), went along "to assist them" (Acts 13:5). In this role, Mark was likely both a teacher in their ministry and also something of a travel secretary for his two older friends.

After crossing Cyprus by land, Paul, Barnabas, and John Mark sailed to the southern coast of Asia Minor, docking at Perga. For reasons unknown, Mark left the mission and returned to Jerusalem. Some students have thought that Mark, being a very young man, may have become homesick. Other have surmised that he resented the fact that Paul had replaced Barnabas as the leader of the mission tour by the time they reached Perga. Mark evidently had been willing to follow Barnabas as the leader, but may not have been willing to accept Paul's leadership. We do not know why Mark left, but we do know that Paul did not like Mark's decision (15:38).

After the first missionary journey ended and the Jerusalem Conference met to give a guideline statement for ministry to the Gentile world, Paul and Barnabas visited Antioch (v. 36). They began to make plans to revisit the cities in Asia Minor where they had proclaimed the gospel on their first journey. Barnabas again wanted to take John Mark with them. Paul, however, disagreed.

According to Luke, "there arose a sharp contention" between Paul and Barnabas over Mark (v. 39). The disagreement must have been severe because the two longtime Christian friends and co-workers "separated from each other" (v. 39). Barnabas took Mark and sailed back to

Cyprus. Paul selected Silas as his new companion, and they went over-
land through Syria and Cilicia to revisit the churches in Asia Minor
(v. 41).

This break in friendship and ministry over John Mark must have been
painful for both Paul and Barnabas. The two men were friends of long
standing. Barnabas had been the first believer to welcome Paul when he
attempted to join the disciples in Jerusalem after his conversion on the
road to Damascus (9:26-27). Shortly thereafter, for his own safety, Paul
went home to Tarsus (vv. 29b-30).

Some time later, Barnabas was sent to Antioch by the Jerusalem
church to investigate further the matter of Gentiles becoming Christian
converts. Arriving in Antioch, Barnabas saw a need which he felt Paul
could help him meet. So Barnabas personally went to Tarsus to find Paul
and bring him back to Antioch to assist in the expanding ministry there
(11:25-26). "For a whole year," Barnabas and Paul worked together in
this church (v. 26). The congregation responded to their leadership, and
Antioch became the most mission-minded church in that area. The disciples were first called "Christians" at Antioch (v. 26).

With such a long-term tie, Barnabas and Paul must have felt keen disappointment as they went their separate ways on the second missionary
journey. To be sure, the great mission cause which they served was not
thwarted. The rift in their friendship over John Mark resulted in two
mission teams going out rather than just one. However, the breach must
have been most unpleasant and difficult.

When Christians sharply disagree, or become petty in their griev-
ances, someone usually gets hurt. Often the cause of Christ is hindered
by such behavior. A web of strained interpersonal relationships almost
always assumes dimensions of sin. Either party in the dispute can self-
ishly insist in having his or her, or their, own way. Too often, the capacity
to reason, remain flexible, and negotiate is lost. Each side tends to become more rigid and determined to hold its own ground. Episodes like
this include domestic squabbles, sibling rivalries, staff conflicts, church
fights, and many other areas of our everyday lives.

Paul and Mark were reconciled, probably a sign of Christian maturity
for both men. Years had passed. Mark was in Rome with Paul (Philem.

24; Col. 4:10). Mark was numbered among the faithful Christian friends who remained with Paul during his difficult imprisonment in Rome.

Sometime during Paul's extended stay in Rome, Mark evidently returned to Asia Minor. In what was probably Paul's last written letter, Mark is mentioned. Paul wrote from Rome to Timothy, who was likely still in Ephesus (1 Tim. 1:3). Paul hoped that Timothy would visit him in Rome (2 Tim. 4:9). He asked Timothy to "get Mark and bring him with you" (v. 11). "For," Paul added, "he is very useful in serving me" (v. 11). That was quite a compliment for Mark from the veteran missionary who once thought that the young man should not be taken on another missionary journey! With the passage of time, Mark had proved himself worthy. He and Paul were again friends and co-workers.

Only limited references indicate healing of the breach in Paul's relationship to Barnabas. Some commentators see Paul's words in 2 Corinthians about the companion to Titus as a reference to Barnabas (8:18-19). In Paul's first letter to the Corinthians, he made a brief, direct reference to Barnabas, which indicates that he and Paul shared similar views about how their ministry was to be supported financially (9:6). Evidently both Barnabas and Paul did much to pay their own way in their missionary endeavors.

Thus we may conclude that Paul had a continuing appreciation for Barnabas and his ministry. The two men may have again engaged in joint labors, especially since Paul was so obviously reconciled with John Mark. With Christian maturity, all three men were able to restore their relationships after such a serious rift. Many of us today could well profit from their example in this regard.

The Sin of Outright Rejection and Unbelief
(Matt. 10:4; Mark 14:10-11; John 6:70-71; 12:1-8; 13:1-30; 18:1-5; Matt. 27:3-10; Acts 1:18-19)

Although he was chosen by Jesus to be a disciple, Judas Iscariot sinned directly against God as he progressively moved toward outright rejection and betrayal of Jesus as the Messiah. The dark passion which drove him to betray the only begotten Son of God is still today largely unfathomable.

What went into the making of Judas Iscariot? He had for his day a very noble name. Judas Maccabeus had been a Jewish national hero. With strong help from his brothers and his father, Judas Maccabeus had led the Jewish people to achieve a brief period of national independence. Remembering that heroic freedom fighter, Jewish boys early in the first century were glad to be named Judas.

The second part of Judas's name—Iscariot—probably referred to the town from whence he came. One of the Hebrew words for man is *ish*. Kerioth was a village in Judah. Thus iscariot—*ish*-Kerioth—likely meant "a man from Kerioth." Judas likely came from Judea in the southern part of the land. All the other disciples and Jesus were from Galilee, in the north.

Jesus spent all night in prayer on the eve of calling His disciples (Luke 6:12-13). The next day, He selected twelve men from those who were then following Him to become His closest associates on earth. Jesus asked Judas to be a disciple, and Judas accepted the invitation. It is a credit to his insight and judgment that he saw in Jesus a great hope for the future.

To be sure, Judas was not included in the inner circle of the twelve. This trio numbered Peter, James, and John, who seemed to act as what we might call the executive committee of the group with Peter serving as the unofficial chairman. Judas was asked, however, to become treasurer of the Twelve (John 13:29). This must have been a recognition of Judas's basic honesty and his administrative ability.

Judas seems to have been a stable person. He never pushed himself forward like James. He did not have the temper of John. He made no rash promises like Peter. He was not a fanatical Jewish patriot like Simon the Zealot, and he was not a collaborator with the Romans like Levi Matthew.

What then went wrong with Judas? With so many good assets in his favor, how did he sink to such depths of evil? Why did he allow his honored name to become an emblem of dishonor and betrayal?

The Gospel writers grappled with this dilemma. Matthew (26:14-16) and Mark (14:10-11) indicated that Judas betrayed Jesus because of greed. To be sure, some money changed hands in the betrayal, but it was only thirty pieces of silver—the price of an injured slave. The amount certainly would not have made Judas wealthy. Luke (22:3) and John (13:2, 27) explained the action of Judas by pointing out that "Satan entered into him" (v. 27). As in Goethe's epic poem, in which Faust sold out to Mephistopheles, so Judas made a deal with the devil and sold out to the prince of this world to destroy Jesus. Judas's betrayal of Jesus was dark, devilish, and demonic. But even for this nefarious deed, we know that the devil did not make him do it!

These two ideas advanced by the Gospel writers plus what we know today about gradual personality development may give the best explanation for Judas's sin. A seed of resentment planted in the human heart, nurtured for years in bitterness, can fester and grow, and later lash out with vicious destruction.

We can mark out some factors that easily could have fed smoldering coals of resentment, which later ignited into flame in Judas's heart. For example, being the only southerner from Judea, when all of the other disciples were from the north in Galilee, Judas could have felt that he was an outsider from the very start. He was not exactly like the eleven other disciples. He didn't share the same background which the others knew.

Furthermore, although he was designated treasurer of the group, Judas was never included with the inner circle of the Twelve. We never read of Peter, James, John, *and Judas* being alone with Jesus. James and John were brothers. Peter's brother, Andrew, also was not named in this smaller group. No resentment over this matter seems to have festered in Andrew's heart, but it may have done so in the attitude of Judas.

An element of greed was a noticeable part of Judas's personality. He was no doubt able with finances, but there is evidence that he also liked to hold the purse strings tight. At the supper in Bethany near the end of Jesus' life, Mary anointed the feet of Jesus with a very expensive perfume (John 12:3). Judas was critical of the extravagance, saying that the perfume might have been sold and the money given to the poor (v. 5). John indicated that Judas said this, not because he really wanted to help the poor, but because he wanted the amount added to the purse, or "money box" (v. 6), which he controlled. John added bluntly that Judas would at times steal from this fund. Jesus rebuked Judas openly. In a statement of his own which probably had a bit of sting in it, Jesus said, "Let her alone, let her keep it for the day of my burial. The poor you always have with you, but you do not always have me" (vv. 7-8).

Later that week, Jesus and all twelve disciples gathered in the upper room in Jerusalem for a solemn observance of the Jewish Passover. In that setting, Jesus instituted the Lord's Supper as the memorial meal of the new covenant. Judas was present for at least a part of the evening. He would have been present during the early part of the evening when Jesus washed the feet of His brash men. Judas saw Jesus filling the role of a common slave.

Jesus somehow did not fulfill Judas's expectations of what the long-expected Messiah should be. Perhaps he thought in terms of a nationalistic, political Messiah who would restore the Davidic throne in Jerusalem. He may have had a dream of seeing what Judas Maccabaeus accomplished only temporarily brought to more permanent fulfillment through Jesus Christ. When it became obvious that Jesus was preparing to die on the cross, Judas's dream would have been shattered. His acute disappointment may have triggered growing resentment that exploded in an impetuous fury which betrayed Jesus into the hands of His enemies.

Whatever the exact dynamic was, the sin of Judas became outright rejection of and disbelief in Jesus. Influenced by background and temperament, goaded by the devil, and disillusioned by false hopes for the future, Judas's traitorous behavior has caused his name to become a synonym for deceit and disloyalty. Jesus said of him, "The Son of man goes as it is written of him, but woe to that man by whom the Son of man is betrayed! It would have been better for that man if he had not been born" (Matt. 26:24).

The most frightening aspect of the sin and death of Judas is that he began so well. Like the other disciples in the twelve, Jesus had called him in all good faith. If we conclude that Judas became a devil in the end, we should also observe that he was not a devil from the beginning. He had every reason and opportunity to know the right and do it. Yet he grievously did wrong.

Herbert Whiting Virgin tells a story about a certain bridge in his native Scotland which may offer further insight as to what went wrong in

Judas's character." Once a massive bridge built by General Wade spanned a deep gorge in the Scottish Highlands. The bridge had been constructed during the Rebellion in order to overawe the Highland clans. Rising above the rocky cliffs of the deep gorge, it was known in that Scottish district as "The High Bridge."

For two hundred years, the bridge had been open for traffic through that area. It was thought to be one of the strongest stone bridges in the country. In one of the periodic government inspections, however, the bridge was pronounced unsafe and closed to heavy traffic. A few years later, the central arch of the bridge collapsed, and the structure fell into the gorge in a kind of inglorious burial.

What caused the destruction of the massive bridge? A tiny birch tree seed caused the downfall. A gust of wind had blown a seed into a fissure above the keystone of the bridge. The seed sank into the moldy lime. It germinated and grew into a sapling, so small at first that a child could have pulled it out. But no child came to do this saving deed. The sapling grew into a tree. Digging its growing roots deeper and deeper into the mortar, the tree ultimately wrenched the solid masonry aside. Devastating cracks ran through the substructure of the bridge, causing damage which could not be repaired. The bridge which stood the blasts of two hundred Scottish winters—a bridge over which armies passed and cannons thundered—succumbed to a tiny seed.

Thus We Conclude

An unforgettable silent interpretation of the life of Judas is found in the magnificent Washington Cathedral in our nation's capital. The prayer rail which divides the congregation from the altar area is supported by twelve wooden statues. These statues—six on either side of the exalted nave—were carved by master craftsmen to depict the lives of the twelve disciples of Jesus. Each handsome wood carving contains some detail which identifies that particular disciple.

When you come to the place where Judas is depicted, you see only a blank, uncarved shaft of wood. This was an artist's way of declaring that Judas is the stark, unfinished character among the disciples.

Sin can leave us stark and unfinished people, separated from God.

Notes

1. Roy L. Honeycutt, Jr., "Exodus," *The Broadman Bible Commentary* (Nashville: Broadman Press, 1969) 1:434.

2. Ibid., p. 435.

3. William H. Morton, "Joshua," *The Broadman Bible Commentary* (Nashville: Broadman Press, 1970) 2:328.

4. Ibid., p. 330.

5. G. G. D. Kilpatrick, *The Interpreter's Bible* (Nashville: Abingdon Press, 1956) 5:201.

6. Frank Stagg, *The Book of Acts* (Nashville: Broadman Press, 1955), p. 82.

7. T. C. Smith, "Acts," *The Broadman Bible Commentary* (Nashville: Broadman Press, 1970) 10:43.

8. Frank Stagg, p. 83.

9. Raymond B. Brown, "First Corinthians," *The Broadman Bible Commentary* (Nashville: Broadman Press, 1970) 10:288.

10. Ibid., p. 323.

11. Quoted by James W. Henley, *His Twelve Apostles* (Book of Methodist sermons with no publisher listed.), pp. 87-88.

6

What About Sin in Christian History?

This volume has primarily been concerned with a study of the doctrine of sin in biblical thought and the reality of sin in contemporary experience. Focus has moved between the world of the Bible and the world today. In our review of sin, we have moved from the world of Moses to the world of Archie Bunker, from the words of Jesus to the words of current Christian laypersons. Such an approach has been a conscious endeavor. Our primary task in Christian discipleship is to pattern our daily lives by the teaching of Jesus and the message of the Bible as a whole.

In pursuing the goal to make the Bible relevant to the world today, however, we are engaged in a kind of space race which moves from the twentieth century back to at least the first century, and then returns to the present. The Old Testament antedates our era by more than two millenia. Most of the New Testament was written nineteen hundred years prior to this decade of the 1980s. So, when we skip from the Bible era to our day, we are bypassing nineteen centuries of Christian thought.

In light of this situation, this chapter examines the idea and understanding of sin in the history of Christian thought. This will be a brief review. Multiple books have been written on this subject. This chapter will summarize what has been taught about sin in Christian history. The four divisions generally considered as major epochs in church history are the early church, the medieval church, the Reformation, and the contemporary or modern era.[1]

Teaching about Sin in the Early Church

What Is the Relationship of Sin to Christian Baptism?

Baptism is older than Christianity. Jesus was baptized by a near kinsman (Luke 1:36), the son of Zechariah and Elizabeth. Because of the emphasis which this man placed upon baptism as a sign of repentance, he is known as John the Baptizer, or John the Baptist.

John inherited the rite of baptism from Judaism. Jewish teaching at the time of Christ required that proselytes, or converts to Judaism, be both circumcized and baptized. Baptism, immersion under water, was an appropriate symbol of the spiritual purification that followed the experience of repentance which John preached. Although Jesus had no need to be washed to be clean from sin, John's baptism did symbolically point toward such a cleansing that came in the wake of genuine repentance.

The baptismal rite itself, however, is older even than John and the Levitical worship. The mystery religions of the ancient Oriental world had similar initiation rites. For example, the religion of Isis and Serapis, which originated in Egypt, included for new believers a cleansing which came from bathing in sacred water. In the cult of Mithraism, which was founded in Persia in the pre-Christian era and became quite popular with Roman soldiers in the second and third centuries, new converts received baptism in the blood of a slain bull—the taurobolium—which they believed caused the initiates to be cleansed and reborn forever.

In his New Testament letters, the apostle Paul made comments which reflect the idea that Christian baptism, in addition to being symbolic of the believer's participation in the death, burial, and resurrection of Christ (Rom. 6:3-5), was also a symbol of the believer's sin being washed away (Acts 22:16; 1 Cor. 6:11; Eph. 5:26; Titus 3:5). Other New Testament writers also referred to this dimension of Christian baptism (Heb. 10:22; 1 Pet. 3:20-21).

Although baptism was important as an act of Christian discipleship (Acts 16:15, 33), Paul did not think that baptism was essential to salvation (1 Cor. 1:14-17). Paul and other New Testament writers often referred to the salvation experience as being complete with no reference to baptism (Rom. 10:8-13; Gal. 2:16; Eph. 2:8-9; Heb. 7:23-25; 1 Pet. 1:3-8).

Soon after the end of the apostolic era, however, the understanding of baptism had grown in importance until early church leaders began to regard it as indispensable to salvation. The ending of Mark's Gospel that is not in the best manuscripts includes this statement: "He who believes and is baptized will be saved" (16:16).

Church leaders in the second century continued to affirm the importance of baptism. Hermas (AD 115-140) commended baptism as the only foundation of the church. Mid-way through the second century, Justin wrote that baptism brought regeneration and illumination to the new Christian. For Tertullian of Carthage in North Africa (c. 155-220), baptism conveyed eternal life itself. Thus, by the end of the second century, Christian writers were generally declaring that baptism washed away all previous sin and that baptism was needed to complete the experience of salvation. Christian baptism was on its way from being viewed as symbol to being seen as sacrament. The way was also being cleared for the forgiveness of sin to be understood as a gift from the church rather than an expression of the grace of God.

What About Sins After Baptism?

The general view of the early church about postbaptismal sins was expressed in the statement from 1 John: "If we confess our sins, he is faithful and just, and will forgive our sins and cleanse us from all unrighteousness" (1:9).

But early Christians also believed that some sins could not be forgiven. These unforgivable sins were usually called "deadly" or "mortal" sins. First John is illustrative at this point: "If any one sees his brother committing what is not a mortal sin, he will ask, and God will give him life for those whose sin is not mortal. There is sin which is mortal; I do not say that one is to pray for that" (5:16). Of course, Jesus Himself had spoken of a sin which could not be forgiven: "Whoever blasphemes against the Holy Spirit never has forgiveness, but is guilty of an eternal sin" (Mark 3:29; see also Matt. 12:32; Luke 12:10).

The general feeling in the postapostolic era of the early church was that the unforgivable sins were idolatry, or denial of the faith; murder; and gross licentiousness. As the Christian faith became a persecuted religion at the hands of Rome, the problem of dealing with those believers who had lapsed from their Christian faith became quite acute.

Gradually the strict interpretation of no "deadly" sins being forgiven after baptism became more relaxed. The idea was advanced by Hermas in the first half of the second century that one further repentance could be granted after baptism. Tertullian taught that after this "second-chance" repentance, no further opportunity for forgiveness could be offered. The second-chance forgiveness was to be given only after a public confession on the part of the sinner. This *exomologesis* was often quite humiliating and emotional.

The question inevitably arose as to when a sinner had done enough to be forgiven and restored. The feeling among some early church leaders in the postapostolic era was that the absolving power was divinely placed in the congregation. Other churchmen, however, believed that power had been given to Peter (Matt. 18:15-18), and by implication, to other church leaders, as church offices developed. In the actual practice of the faith, many ordinary Christians came to feel that persons about to be martyred and confessors could hear confession and forgive sin. Confessors were Christians who had endured persecution for their faith and prevailed.

One such confessor, a man by the name of Kallistos, became bishop of Rome early in the third century (217-222). He issued a declaration in his own name, which became a landmark decision as the power of papal authority was later to develop. Kallistos declared that he himself would absolve sins of the flesh on a proper repentance from the offender. Not even Kallistos, however, would grant pardon for those who had lapsed, or forsaken, their Christian faith.

Before the third century closed, however, synods meeting in Carthage and Rome voted to permit the restoration of the lapsed, under strict conditions of penance. The idea persisted in the minds of many of the faithful, however, that the best way to handle post-baptismal sins was to delay being baptized. A most notable example of this practice is seen in the fact that Constantine, the first Roman emperor to become a Christian believer, was not baptized until he was on his deathbed in 337.

How Is Sin Transmitted?

As Christian thought became more developed and reflective about the nature of sin and its pervasive work in human nature, some concern emerged as to how sin is transmitted. How does the contagion of sin pass from one generation to the next? How do the fathers eat sour grapes and set their children's teeth on edge? (See Ezek. 18:2; Jer. 31:29.)

Certain biblical passages had pivotal influence on developing Christian thought. For example, in one of the pentitential psalms, by strong tradition attributed to David, the psalmist declared: "Behold, I was brought forth in iniquity, and in sin did my mother conceive me" (51:5). That does not imply that the psalmist was illegitimate, or of ignoble birth. It does affirm that sin is a deep infection of the whole of human nature. Sin was not viewed as being primarily learned behavior. As A. F. Kirkpatrick commented on this verse, individual "acts of sin have their root in the inherited sinfulness of mankind."[2] But the question remained—how is this infection or inheritance passed from parent to child, from person to person?

This concern, or theme, also appears in the writing of Paul. In a key statement defending the resurrection of Jesus and upholding the Christian hope in the resurrection of believers, Paul declared, "For as by a man came death, by a man has come also the resurrection of the dead. For as in Adam all die, so also in Christ shall all be made alive" (1 Cor. 15:21-22).

In another passage, which is very personal and autobiographical, Paul described what we might call the all-pervasive nature of sin in man's heart:

> I do not understand my own actions. For I do not do what I want, but I do the very thing I hate. Now if I do what I do not want, I agree that the law is good. So then it is no longer I that do it, but sin which dwells within me. For I know that nothing good dwells within me, that is, in my flesh. I can will what is right, but I cannot do it. For I do not do the good I want, but the evil I do not want is what I do. Now if I do what I do not want, it is no longer I that do it, but sin which dwells within me (Rom. 7:15-20).

We can say with Paul that sin is present in our lives, but the question remains, How did it get there?

Writing in the second century, Irenaeus (c. 125-200) of Asia Minor and Lyons (Gaul) developed Paul's idea of the first and second Adam. Through God's creation, the first Adam was both good and immortal. But in Adam's disobedience in Eden, he lost both his natural goodness and his immortality. This initial loss in the disobedience of Adam became the legacy of all mankind. Man could no longer be considered naturally good. All people were also destined to die. But how this inheritance was transferred, Irenaeus did not say.

Church historians generally consider Tertullian of Carthage, writing early in the third century, to be the Christian thinker who had a deeper sense of sin than any Christian writer since Paul. Tertullian greatly influenced the development of the concept of sin in the Latin, or Western, church.

Tertullian did not think that good and evil in man could be accounted for by different natural endowments. If evil were in man's nature, it would be impossible to pass moral judgment upon him. Tertullian looked upon man as being naturally endowed with independence. Human sin was, thus, a free act of man. To be good was to obey God. In contrast to this, to be evil was to disobey God. Such sin was a disobedience which brings death.

Tertullian said that in Adam the whole race was disobedient. That expressed idea later came to be known as the doctrine of original sin. He spoke of evil as being a "blemish of origin" in man. He wrote of "the corruption of nature" as becoming "second nature" to man. He spoke of a "birthmark of sin." In all of this, however, he maintained man's freedom of will. In other words, for Tertullian, in spite of Adam's sin, any given man could choose not to sin.[3]

Another North African churchman, Augustine of Hippo, refined and made conclusive the idea of original sin. Augustine is a towering figure in church history. Williston Walker wrote of him, "In Augustine the ancient church reached its highest religious attainment since apostolic times."[4]

The wide range of Augustine's thought touched almost every area of Christian doctrine in his time, and his voice continues to influence vital areas of Christian thought today. Perhaps Augustine is best known for his teaching on the doctrine of man and the problem of good and evil. Not only did he write important treatises in this area, but he also wrote a detailed account of his own pilgrimage in life and faith. This work, entitled *Confessions,* stands as a classic example of authentic spiritual autobiography.

According to Augustine, man was created good and upright. Man was initially endowed by God with free will, which included the possibility of not sinning and knowing immortality. In that state, man was happy and in communion with God. From that idyllic bliss, however, Adam, the first man, fell by sin. Augustine regarded pride as the essence of sin, that is man's ability to proudly set himself up, over, and above the expressed will of God.

In sinful pride, man's possibility of doing good was lost. God's grace was forfeited, and the soul became subject to death. Adam fell into a hopeless state of ruin and ultimate death.

Interpreting from Paul's Letter to the Romans, Augustine concluded that in Adam's initial sin all people were involved. All mankind shared in Adam's loss of the possibility of doing good and experiencing immortality. The result was and is that the whole human race, even to the youngest infant, is a "mass of perdition." From this hopeless state of original sin, Augustine wrote that "no one, no, not one, has been delivered, or is being delivered, or ever will be delivered, except by the grace of the Redeemer."[5]

In the development of his thought, Augustine placed the locus of sin in the will of man. Three stages may be noted in his understanding of the nature of sin and evil.[6] He first set forth his concept of evil in terms of Manichaean dualism. Here the seat of sin was posited outside the soul or self in the world of matter. With this viewpoint, sin is essentially seen as sensuality. The basic contradiction in man lies in the created body rather than in the inner soul or heart. Thus understood, sin would be transmitted physically.

Commentators today who say that sin is transmitted through the male sperm reflect, perhaps unknowingly, this sort of dualist viewpoint. Such must be considered a very surface view of the human tragedy of sin.

At a second stage in his thought under the influence of Neoplatonism,

Augustine defined sin and evil in terms of negation, or privation, of the good. Here sin was set forth in terms of finitude, or creatureliness. Evil is the limitation or the absence of being. Evil is non-being. Augustine came to recognize, however, a disintegrating force in man which defies analysis merely in terms of finitude.

The more mature Augustine, in a third stage, found the locus of sin in man's inner being. The soul or the self is the seat of sin. The origin of sin is in neither the creation nor in the Creator, but in the will of man. Sin is not caused by the flesh; it is caused by the spirit. Willful pride is the cause of sin. With such pride, man always chooses to love himself rather than live in obedient love with God. This was the original sin of Adam and Eve, and it is also the original sin of every other person.

In a long-standing controversy with the Irish monk Pelagius, Augustine successfully defended his thought that it was impossible for anyone to choose not to sin. Thus writing early in the fifth century, Augustine upheld the biblical doctrine that no one is naturally righteous (Ps. 14:1-2; 53:1-2; Rom. 3:9-23).

This understanding of sin points to the fact that all of us live in a world of mirrors. Every direction we turn, we see reflected the extension of our own image and self-interest. All of us initially live in a big "I" world, with little concern for any other "Thou"—that is, any other person. Augustine believed this kind of behavior was perhaps most clearly and consistently seen in the thoughtlessly selfish behavior of babies. He defined one of the psychological dimensions of sin as "infantilism." He also described sin psychologically in terms of animalism, diabolism, and flight from reality. The grace of God through Jesus Christ transforms our mirrors into windows, whereby we see the world of other people. Ultimately, for Christians, the windows should become doors through which the transformed believer goes forth to serve and minister to the needs of other people in the name of Jesus Christ.

The early postapostolic church took individual sin seriously. The understanding of sin and the understanding of the meaning of baptism were closely aligned in the life and work of the church. The problem of dealing with those who had "lapsed" from the faith was a major concern. In the first Christian centuries, a movement can be traced in which the understanding of Christian baptism changed from being a meaningful symbol of salvation toward becoming an obligatory sacrament necessary for salavation. Late in this period, the writings of Augustine affirmed the original sinfulness of all mankind. The locus of sin was placed in the heart, or will, of man. Some of these patterns of thought were set even more decisively during the Middle Ages.

Teaching about Sin in the Medieval Church

The beginning date for the medieval period of European history is debated by scholars.[7] Some suggest a date as early as 312-313, when Emperor Constantine recognized Christianity as the official religion of the Roman Empire. Rather than being destroyed by imperial Rome, the Christian faith survived and triumphed over Roman persecution. Other scholars prefer to date the Middle Ages from the year 476, which is considered to be the time of the fall of the Roman Empire. After repeated invasions by the barbarians in the north, Odovacar the Ostrogoth sacked Rome and the emperor abdicated that year.

Still other historians date the origin of the medieval period from Christmas Day in the year 800. At that time, the Frankish king, Charles the Great—Charlemagne—received the imperial Roman crown from Pope Leo III in Saint Peter's Church in Rome. The intention was to recreate the Pax Romana (Roman peace) of the old Roman Empire, but instead the ceremony ushered in a new concept of emerging Western Europe.

In the vacuum created by the fall of Rome, the church survived as the strongest social entity. The rise of Islam in the East, with its martial dominance of all of North Africa and the Mediterranean Sea, caused the Christian church to be cut off from its earlier strong home bases in Palestine, Egypt, and Asia Minor. Western Europe became a feudal society with larger city-states and feudal lords vying for dominance.

The church became the strongest controlling influence in society. The church, or cathedral, dominated not only the skyline of most medieval towns of Europe but also the lives of the people. And the city of Rome became a ruling force among the churches—not through an emperor, but through the Pope. At the height of its power under Innocent III, the papacy in Rome could crown kings, depose princes, appoint bishops, and burn heretics—without answering to any other authority. The teaching of the medieval church about sin can best be understood against the backdrop of this total social milieu.

How Did the Relationship Between Sin and Baptism Become More Formalized in the Medieval Church?

By the postapostolic era, baptism was regarded as necessary to complete the experience of salvation. This idea and the view of original sin led to the practice of infant baptism and the view of baptism as a sacrament in the Middle Ages.

The first mention of infant baptism is found in the writing of Irenaeus of Lyons about 185.[8] Writing a bit later, early in the third century, Tertullian also spoke specifically of the practice, but he discouraged its use. Tertullian preferred to delay baptism until a candidate's character was more fully formed. Later in the same century, both Cyprian of Carthage (200-258) and Origen of Alexandria (c. 182-251) favored infant baptism. Origen considered infant baptism an apostolic custom, and Cyprian argued for the practice from his idea of original sin.

Although there is no certain evidence as to why the practice of infant baptism arose, the latent ideas which resulted in the practice seem rather clear. The rite of baptism was thought to wash away sin. Sin is one way or another is with us from our birth. Infant mortality rates were high. Sincere Christian parents did not want to risk their children failing to enter the kingdom of God. So, the practice grew. By the sixth century, or in the early Middle Ages, this rite had become universal in the church.

In providing the rite of baptism for the people, the church also became the dispenser of salvation. Baptism was seen, not as a sacred symbol of spiritual cleansing and death, burial, and resurrection faith, but as a solemn sacrament whereby salvation was actually mediated to the recipient. To be baptized by the church was to be saved and given entry into the kingdom of God. For the church to withhold, or deny, baptism was to cause a person to be lost forever.

Baptism was but one sacrament administered by the medieval church. During the twelfth century, seven sacraments were administered by the church. This was largely due to the work of Peter Lombard—a prominent churchman who, though born in northern Italy, is primarily remembered as a teacher of theology in the school of Notre Dame and as the Bishop of Paris (c. 1147-1159).

As enumerated by Peter Lombard, the sacraments were baptism, confirmation, the Lord's Supper (or the Mass), matrimony, ordination, penance, and extreme unction. Since baptism was performed at birth and extreme unction at the time of death, the sacraments came to be known as a kind of ecclesiastical insurance whereby a person could be covered "from womb to tomb"!

A positive word can be said for this sacramental system. During the Middle Ages, the church in Western Europe was trying to minister to a populace which was largely illiterate. Services of the church, including the Mass, were in Latin—which was no longer the spoken language of the people. Likewise, the scroll-copied editions of the Bible were largely unavailable to the common people. They were too few, too expensive, and also too removed from the language which the people used.

The sacramental system developed as a sincere attempt by medieval churchmen to bring a Christian influence to bear on the lives of their people at the most significant events or crises of their lives: birth, conversion, worship, marriage, vocation, sin and guilt, and death. These areas are typical of life crises for individuals today. With sensitive Christian sharing and pastoral care, we still seek to bring the presence of God in Christ to bear on the lives of our friends as they pass through these major human epochs. A primary difference between now and then, however, is that our ministry in these areas is more personal and voluntary, as we seek to be instruments and channels for God's amazing grace. In the medieval church, this ministry was more structured and obligatory, with the church itself being seen as the mediator of the healing or forgiving grace. Such authority and power, in time, allowed the church to become very heavy-handed in the manner whereby the sacraments were given or withheld, as the case might be.

How Did the Sacrament of Penance Develop in the Medieval Church?

Sin and guilt are universal and timeless human problems. The sacrament of penance sought to address this ageless concern. What was initially a valid idea based on the biblical teaching relative to the confession of sin (Ps. 51:1-12,15-17; 32:1-5; John 3:6; Jas. 5:16; 1 John 1:8-10), quickly became an impersonal, obligatory, formalized ritual which imparted forgiveness through the auspices of the church rather than by the grace of God.

The early church had wrestled with the matter of what to do about postbaptismal sin. As infant baptism became well established in church practice early during the Middle Ages, the concern of what to do about postbaptismal sin became acute. Most people were dealing with a lifetime of postbaptismal sin. The idea of penance emerged to meet this need.

Although it was never considered a sacrament of equal dignity with baptism and the Lord's Supper, penance was of prime importance in medieval church practice. "The Latin mind has always been inclined to view sin and righteousness in terms of definite acts rather than as states, and therefore to look upon man's relations to God under the aspects of debt and credit."[9] This sentiment became fertile soil in which the idea of penance grew to full fruition in the Middle Ages.

The practice of private confession by both clerical and laypersons had been introduced to Europe early in the seventh century by Irish monks who were working as missionaries. The Irish monk Columbanus is much associated with the introduction of the practice of confession.

Six hundred years later, in 1215, what had begun as a voluntary matter of personal Christian discipline was decreed to be church law by the Fourth Lateran Council. This decision required confession to a priest at least once a year of all laymen of the age of discretion. This law prescribed that on evidence of sorrow for sin, confession, and a willingness to give satisfaction, a priest, as God's minister, could pronounce absolution. Without priestly pardon, no person guilty of a deadly sin after baptism could have assurance of salvation.

Thomas Aquinas was the medieval theologian who more fully developed various dimensions of the sacrament of penance. He wrote that penance involved four elements: contrition, confession, satisfaction, and absolution. Contrition was sincere sorrow for any offense against God and the determination not to do it again. Confession was the act of speaking directly to a priest, as prescribed by church law. Absolution was the cleansing and forgiveness which was granted by the priest.

At the point of "satisfaction," the sacrament of penance became most vulnerable to exploitation. Aquinas and other medieval churchmen taught that although God forgives eternal punishment through penance, certain temporal penalties may remain as a result of sin. These temporal penalties would "satisfy" the seriousness of the offense against God, so far as that was possible. The priest imposed these satisfactions.

Certain churchmen began to rationalize, however, that there was a way whereby these temporal penalties could be removed. Such remission came to be called an "indulgence." The idea of indulgences opened the door to much ecclesiastical graft and corruption. Indulgences, or removing the temporal penalties of sin, could be bought by monetary favors to the church. Giving land for building a monastery, contributing money for the erection of a church, constructing a road or bridge to aid churchmen in their travel—these and many other projects were employed as ways to purchase indulgences. The French pope, Urban II (1088-1099), for example, recruited an army by promising full indulgence for all persons who became a part of the First Crusade to free the Holy Land from the Muslims.

In the medieval church, the understanding of sin and forgiveness became less personal and direct in relationship to God and more institutional and mechanical in relationship to the church. Early in this period, infant baptism became the established rite whereby the blight of original sin was washed away under the direct auspices of the church. In good faith, sincere churchmen tried to bring a Christian influence to bear upon the lives of parishioners when most of these people could not read or write. The ultimate result was the emergence of the system of seven sacraments.

In time, however, rather than being a means for the church to minister to its people, the sacramental system became a means whereby the church controlled its people. At the height of its power in this era, the Papacy in Rome was the largest landowner in Europe, and the pope himself was the wealthiest prince.

As the sacrament of penance came to be practiced in the later Middle Ages, the church opened its doors to gross graft and corruption. The stage was fully set for a much-needed reformation.

Teaching About Sin in the Reformation Period

The pendulum of history swings slowly. Change does occur, however, as old eras fade and new eras dawn. The streams of thought and events which came together to move Western civilization out of the Middle Ages into the new age of the Renaissance and Reformation were many. For example, one of the lasting effects of the Crusades by European Christians was the reopening of the Mediterranean Sea. Having been essentially landlocked at its southern shore for centuries, Europe began to experience a growing exchange of both goods and ideas from the East.

Economically, the Western world was moving from a barter system to a monetary system for the exchange of goods. Coinage and banking were definitely on the rise. An emerging sense of national pride also marked the period. The presence of the Roman Catholic Church was known throughout Europe, but people were becoming more aware of their specific national origins.

The intellectual ferment of the time was enriched by the rediscovery of languages and literature from the East, including Greek, Arabic, and Hebrew. The rich heritage of Greek culture was unearthed, causing a general renaissance, or rebirth, in classical learning. In time, texts of the Bible became available in their original languages. Jerome's monumental translation, the Latin Vulgate, began to become somewhat obsolete, as people began to want to read God's word in their own tongue.

Another sign of the times was the growing sense of unrest and disillusionment with many practices of the Roman Church. Papal taxation and interference with clerical appointments were generally deemed oppressive. The clergy in local parishes were much criticized for the unworthy examples which many of them gave—both in high station and low. Monasteries were in sore need of reform, and both princes and peasants resented the large landed estates which were held by the monastic orders.

The most direct way, however, whereby most people felt the continual presence of the church in their lives revolved around the sacrament of penance and the sale of indulgences. By the turn of the sixteenth century, indulgences had become more than a primary manner of dispensing forgiveness of sin. They were also a primary tool for raising church revenues. Roland Bainton commented that indulgences "were the bingo of the sixteenth century."[10] So scandalous had this practice become that one preacher of that day redefined the requisites for penance as three: contrition, confession, and *contribution*.

Did Buying an Indulgence Actually Secure the Forgiveness of Sin?

Leo X, of the Italian house of Medici, was elected pope in 1513. He became very interested in completing the new basilica of Saint Peter's in Rome. The old wooden church, built in the time of Constantine, had been condemned. Pope Julius II had started a new church, but his work was left unfinished. Pope Leo wanted to complete the job, but to do so he needed vast amounts of money.

Leo X brought forth the idea of issuing a new "plenary" indulgence. This would be a full and perfect remission of all sin. Subscribers to this indulgence would be restored to the state of innocence which they enjoyed in baptism. They would be released from all the pains of purgatory. Indulgence in behalf of the dead already in purgatory would also be offered.

Various commissioners were appointed and assigned to sell these indulgences all across Europe. Johann Tetzel, a Dominican monk of clever eloquence, went to the area of Germany where Martin Luther lived. Tetzel preached sermons to promote the sale of indulgences. In one he said:

> Consider that all who are contrite and have confessed and made contribution will receive complete remission of all their sins. Listen to the voices of your dear dead relatives and friends, beseeching you and saying, "Pity us, pity us. We are in dire torment from which you can redeem us for a pittance." Do you not wish to? Open your ears. Hear the father

saying to his son, the mother to her daughter, "We bore you, nourished you, brought you up, left you our fortunes, and you are so cruel and hard that now you are not willing for so little to set us free. Will you let us lie here in flames? Will you delay our promised glory?"

Remember that you are able to release them, for

As soon as the coin in the coffer rings,
The soul from purgatory springs.

Will you not then for a quarter of a florin receive these letters of indulgence through which you are able to lead a divine and immortal soul into the fatherland of paradise?[11]

Such crass commercialism in the name of Christ was almost certain to call forth a negative response from some of the people who heard. Such was the case for Martin Luther, an Augustinian monk who was teaching at the University of Wittenberg in east Germany. Luther had been teaching courses in the Psalms and in Paul's Letter to the Romans. He had rediscovered Paul's understanding of sin and forgiveness. The plenary indulgence of Pope Leo X violated everything Luther was finding in the Bible.

On October 31, 1517, the Eve of All Saints' Day, Luther nailed his ninety-five theses to the door of the Castle Church in Wittenberg. The door of the church was like a large public bulletin board. These were ninety-five questions or propositions which Luther wanted to discuss openly with church leaders.

Luther did not initially intend to start a reformation movement. He saw abuses in church practice which he thought needed correction, but he did not begin with the idea of breaking with Rome. To be sure, he and many of his peers did not like the idea of German money going to build an Italian church in Rome. The root of his concern, however, was not economic; it was theological and religious.

The sale of indulgences, and the whole idea surrounding sin and forgiveness as taught by the Roman Church at that time, was foreign to the teaching of the Bible. The center of Luther's thought was "the affirmation of the forgiveness of sins through the utterly unmerited grace of God made possible by the cross of Christ, which reconciled wrath and mercy, routed the hosts of hell, triumphed over sin and death, and by the resurrection manifested that power which enables man to die to sin and rise to newness of life."[12] These ideas, of course, are at the heart of Paul's theology. The Reformation was, thus, based on the New Testament teaching on sin and forgiveness.

How Did Other Leaders in the Reformation View Sin and Forgiveness?

Luther's voice from Wittenberg was heard all across Europe. The spirit of reform blowing across Europe in the early 1500s touched many men. The Reformation leaders were not duplicates of one another, but they shared similarities, as well as differences.

One of these Swiss Reformers was Ulrich Zwingli, who was born on January 1, 1484, in the little township of Wildhaus—the highest village at that time in the Toggenburg Valley.[13] By 1519, Zwingli had moved to Zurich, which became the center of his ministry and activity until his untimely death in 1531.

Zwingli is primarily remembered in Christian thought for his interpretation of the Lord's Supper, which went further than the other prominent Reformers in restoring the supper to its New Testament setting and simplicity. He saw the bread and the wine of the supper as *symbolic elements,* pointing to Christ's death on the cross for the sins of all people. This straightforward biblicism is indicative of the Reformation spirit, which cut back through centuries of church tradition to rediscover the authentic word of the Bible. Like the other Reformers, Zwingli emphasized the religious and personal character of sin, as seen in light of the biblical revelation.

Another Swiss Reformer of even greater importance was John Calvin (1509-1564). Although Calvin was actually French by birth—the family name was Cauvin—he is considered a Swiss Reformer because his major ministry was in Geneva. Calvin fled from France while still in his twenties because of his evangelical conversion experience and his sympathies with Protestant views. He initially found a haven in Basel, Switzerland, which had become a Protestant town.

Calvin, a very good student, had been trained in law, but he also studied extensively in theology and the classic humanities. He was a careful student of Greek and Hebrew. When Calvin was twenty-six years old he wrote a book, *The Institutes of the Christian Religion,* which became the primer for Protestantism.

Calvin went to Geneva in 1536, working as a lecturer on the Bible. He was appointed as a preacher a year later. Calvin became the dominant influence in the whole city. Geneva became a type of theocratic society, with life organized almost totally around the Protestant church. Calvin's was the only system the Reformation produced that could organize itself successfully in the face of strong government opposition. Thus his religious ideas were felt in many countries throughout Europe, and ultimately in the New World. Calvin became the most "international" of all the sixteenth-century Reformers.

Calvin's view of sin and the forgiveness of sin may be briefly summarized as follows:

> Man's highest knowledge . . . is that of God and of himself. Enough comes by nature to leave man without excuse, but adequate knowledge is given only in the Scriptures, which the witness of the Spirit in the heart of the believing reader attests as the very voice of God. These Scriptures teach that God is good, and the source of all goodness everywhere. Obedience to God's will is man's primal duty. As originally created, man was good and capable of obeying God's will, but he lost goodness and power alike in Adam's fall, and is now, of himself, absolutely incapable of goodness. Hence no work of man's can have any merit; and all men are in a state of ruin meriting only damnation. From this helpless and hopeless condition some men are undeservedly rescued through the work of Christ. He paid the penalty due for the sins of those in whose behalf He died; yet the offer and reception of this ransom was a free act on God's part, so that its cause is God's love.[14]

Current Christian thought in regard to sin and God's forgiveness has been greatly influenced by the legacy of John Calvin.

Another Reformation movement came to be known by a descriptive title rather than by an individual man's name. This was the Anabaptist movement. These Christians believed that infant baptism was not valid scriptural baptism. In light of this conviction, they were rebaptized, or baptized again—"anabaptism"—as adult believers. They believed that the other Reformers were going only halfway in their efforts to restore the church to its New Testament setting and simplicity.

Anabaptists also believed in the separation of church and state, which would allow congregations to be self-governing bodies, independent of state or episcopal control. Involvement in civil affairs was considered a sin. They placed great emphasis upon the Bible as the sole sufficient rule for faith and practice. Many Anabaptist congregations followed an ascetic life-style, trying to live in strict conformity to their understanding of biblical requirements. Some groups became pacificists and would not go to war nor swear by any oath.

Anabaptist groups first appeared in Switzerland and Germany—somewhat in the wake of the other reformations in progress. From there, they spread to the Netherlands and England, and ultimately to the New World.

Early leaders among the Anabaptists were Conrad Grebel and Felix Manz in Zurich, and Balthasar Hubmaier in Waldshut, a small village in the northern edge of Switzerland. On February 7, 1525, a group of Anabaptists reinstituted believer's baptism in a private home in a town near Zurich. This particular baptism was done by sprinkling. A few weeks later, however, in similar service, believers were baptized by immersion. Anabaptist views greatly influenced several other religious groups such as the Mennonites, the Hutterites, the Amish, as well as Quakers, Baptists, and Congregationalists.

Primarily because of their views on the limited authority of the state, Anabaptists groups at times experienced severe persecution. Many of their early leaders were martyred—often by drowning because of their emphasis upon believers baptism by immersion.

Many other pivotal churchmen from this era could be named: John Knox in Scotland; Thomas Helwys, John Smyth, and George Fox in England. Although his motivation was not primarily religious, King Henry VIII played a crucial role in the English Reformation, which gave birth to the Anglican Church.

In response to the crass commercialism and exploitation of the medieval Catholic Church, and in the wake of the new learning associated with the Renaissance, a strong desire to return to the Bible emerged in early sixteenth-century Europe. The history of the church in the Western world in time was dramatically altered. Bible concepts replaced the dogma of church councils as the authoritative source for finding Christian truth. Sin and forgiveness came to be understood not in terms of papal decrees, but by the straightforward language of the Bible.

Teaching About Sin in the Modern Era

Gigantic changes took place in man's total life-style as he moved from the Reformation to the modern era. His concept of the physical world changed from believing the earth was flat to believing he can travel in space. His work has changed from manual farm labor to mechanical industrial assembly lines. Man has moved from a world of self-sustaining families to a world family where many members face starvation. While man in the Reformation era feared local feudal uprisings, modern man faces the possible destruction of worldwide civilization by nuclear war.

Inevitably these changes have affected man's understanding of himself and his world view of right and wrong. Entrance into the modern era brought a greater in-depth perception of man's human predicament. It is to this understanding of sin that we would now direct our attention.

Has Any Dimension of Sin Been Brought into Sharper Focus in the Modern Era?

An awareness of the individual, personal dimension of sin was never totally lost among Christians in this era. It was the primary view of sin inherited from sixteen centuries of Christian thought. For example, the list of the seven deadly sins was codified by the time of Pope Gregory the Great (540-604). This catalog of sin is commonly identified by the catchword, *saligia,* which is an acrostic made up of the initial letters from the Latin titles for each vice named in the seven deadly sins.[15] These sins are: *superbia* (pride), *avaritia* (covetousness), *luxuria* (lust), *invidia* (envy), *gula* (gluttony), *ira* (anger), *accedia* (sloth).

Although some social, or group, aspects of these seven sins might be noted, by and large they point to areas of sinful behavior which are singular and personal. The individual person was at the center of the popular Christian mind-set regarding sin. Individuals were capable of making personal moral decisions. Consequently, they were ethically responsible for their actions.

A marked emphasis in the modern era, however, pointed to man's progressive loss of a sense of individual identity. A loss in identity awareness contributed to a loss in one's sense of responsibility. Farm life had placed a priority on self-reliance and individual initiative. Life in the town, and even more life in the secular city, tended to herd people together so that individual personhood could easily be lost in the crowd.

A worker on the farm tended to see a product in his area of life from the beginning to the end. A farmer lived with his crops from seedtime to harvest. He experienced a real sense of achievement when his work was finished. On the other hand, a worker in a factory tended to see only an isolated sequence in the manufacturing process on which he was working. The joy of initiating a new idea and bringing it to final completion as a finished product was not as clearly perceived by the factory worker. In this partial loss of his sense of achievement, the worker also lost a vital part of himself. Mass production was increasingly done by mass men.

Mass man tends to become more a number than a person. He becomes more a statistic than a soul. Mass man begins to gain his primary identity from the group, or groups, to which he belongs. Mass man is a WASP, a Catholic, a Black, a Hispanic, a part of the management team, a union worker, a nonunion worker. Vast systems tend to gain control of mass men, so that the right of individual moral choice becomes blurred, or even lost, in the sea of modern bureaucracy.

Who is responsible for the delinquency of a youth in the ghetto who has lived there all of his life because his father is continually in and out of work, unable to provide even a meager standard of living? Who is responsible when a workman—who has been laid off from work because a machine now does his job—steals to feed his family or takes his own life so his family may collect his life insurance benefits? Who is responsible in this highly mobile industrial society—which allows the open sale of alcohol as a beverage—when a drunk driver plows his truck into a loaded school bus, killing several children? However these questions are answered, the social dimension of sin has become much more obvious in our modern industrial society.

A concern known as the Social Gospel movement became much a part of the modern era. Incisive theologians like Ernst Troeltsch, Walter Rauschenbush, Richard Niebuhr, and Reinhold Niebuhr, sought to call forth our involvement in the implications of the gospel for society at large.

The Social Gospel movement was rightly criticized when its proponents sought to redeem society with a humanitarian emphasis which left little place for God and religious faith. But also to be judged inadequate was the simplistic ethic of a Christian piety which emphasized saving souls, with no regard for changing the environment in which those same souls had to live out their lives.

Responsible Christian discipleship today tends to see this issue not as an either-or choice, but as a both-and imperative. Men who have been saved and changed by a personal encounter with God through Jesus Christ ought to become light on a hill and leaven in the lump, as they guide and penetrate the whole social structure. This blending of individual, evangelical faith with genuine concern for society is one of the hallmarks of the Christian view of sin and salvation in the modern era.

Did Any Sharp Reversal in Thought Relative to Sin Occur in This Era?

We should give careful attention to late nineteenth- and early twentieth-century thought and events in answering this question. The latter decades of the nineteenth century were filled with a strong international sense of progress. Man's life on the earth was becoming so much easier than earlier generations had experienced. Modern medicine was making great strides in conquering diseases which had afflicted mankind for centuries. Great labor-saving devices were removing much of man's drudgery and expenditure of human energy in doing daily work. The standard of living for millions of families was being raised as mass-produced goods became available on a broad scale to the general population.

In the midst of this rapid expansion of the benefits of the industrial revolution to ever-increasing numbers of people, some observers began to think that mankind was riding an escalator of inevitable progress that would know no limits. A modern-day utopia seemed to be just on the horizon—certainly within man's grasp with a further bit of heroic effort.

Philosophers and theologians, teachers and preachers, were affected by this spirit of optimism. Man was making such moral progress that some people began to think that man just might outgrow sin and moral evil. The goodness of human nature was strongly affirmed. The idea of sin, in some circles, was going out of style. Some thoughtful observers expressed it this way: Man was turning the cruel, cold world into a lovely glass palace, which was open, airy, and secure.

This idyllic mood of well-being was rudely punctured by the destructive years of World War I, 1914-1918. Suddenly the fruit of mass production was used to wreak havoc on the enemy. Alfred Nobel, the Swedish scientist, had hoped that his discovery of dynamite in 1867 would be a blessing to mankind. But World War I proved that Nobel's discovery only aided some men in building more destructive bombs and bullets.

The world was still recovering from the war years when still another devastating event occurred. In late 1929, almost eleven years to the day from the date of the armistice which ended World War I, the stock market in New York City crashed. This nation and the world plunged into the greatest economic depression that had ever been known. Many men lost fortunes overnight, dropping from the high and mighty to the poor and lowly in a matter of hours. Millions of other people lost their jobs. Bread lines and soup kitchens sprang up all over the world.

The world was still trying to recover from the depression of the early 1930s when Adolph Hitler's Third Reich invaded Poland on September 1, 1939. The date was just a decade from the beginning of the depression. World War II brought even greater destructive weaponry to bear on human life and property. The war years of the 1940s ended after devastating atomic bombs were dropped on the Japanese cities of Hiroshima and Nagasaki. In the early postwar years, the world was shocked to learn of Nazi atrocities against the Jews, which has come to be known as the Holocaust. The Nazis added a horrible new chapter to the tragically painful story of man's inhumanity to man.

In the wake of such slaughter and destruction in the first half of this century, man's utopian glass palace was shattered. Talk about the goodness of man was lost as a generation had to deal with the destruction and madness of war and economic collapse. The industrial revolution had not changed man's heart. It had only placed in his hands products which were more lethally powerful than any previous generation had known.

Men began to talk again about the basic sinfulness of man and his need for redemption. What is known as the neoorthodox movement came to the front in theology, with thinkers like Emil Brunner, Karl Barth, Reinhold Niebuhr,, and others reminding us that man first, last, and foremost is a sinner!

Can Any Correlation Be Made Between the Concept of Both Personal and Corporate Sin in the Modern Era and Sin in the Bible?

The answer to such a question is a strong affirmative. The primary view of sin in the Scripture is that it involves personal disobedience, rebellion, immorality, which is an offense to God. From the biblical point of view, man can never pass the buck and imply that his own sin is the direct responsibility of some other person or group.

Jesus dealt with people on a personal basis. Matthew at his seat of custom or the woman at Jacob's well in Samaria or Nicodemus coming to see Jesus at night or Nathaniel sitting under a fig tree—Jesus called people to discipleship very singularly. As the words of a children's chorus unforgettably declare, "Jesus called them one by one—Peter, Andrew, James, and John."

A strong sense of corporate identity and social interrelatedness is also found in the Bible. From the very outset in Eden, the biblical narrative reports that Eve ate of the fruit which God had placed off limits. Then she "gave some to her husband, and he ate" (Gen. 3:6). Adam was responsible for his decision to eat the forbidden fruit, but Eve certainly encouraged and influenced him to do so. In Cain's destruction of Abel (4:1-16), we are taught that we have a responsibility to and for one another. In a profound sense, we are our brothers' keepers.

This initial sound echoes throughout the Bible. Through the mutual interaction of Aaron and the Israelites, while Moses was on Mount Sinai receiving the Decalogue, they were on the plain making a golden calf for pagan worship (Ex. 32:1-10). While David was seducing Bathsheba and arranging to have Uriah killed, his own children were following his devious example with their own gross immorality and violence. While Gomer was pursuing her lovers, the heart of her husband, Hosea, was strained to the breaking point. In a strange reversal of roles, it was Gomer's children who didn't know where their mother was! Such a list of biblical examples of sin and sinners could be greatly extended.

We sin as individuals, but we never sin alone. We do our sin in some kind of community—the family, the neighborhood, the city, the world. Someone else is always affected by our sin. Furthermore, we can never pay the price of redemption from our sin. Some other person, or group, always has to pay the price for our sin. Thus, the renewed emphasis on the social aspect of sin which we have noted in the modern period can be directly correlated with insight and perception which we also find in the Bible.

Thus We Conclude

In summary, from the discussion in the early church of the relationship between Christian baptism and sin, to the problems of acid rain and city ghettos today, concern about human sin is a thread which runs through twenty centuries of Christian thought. Sin is more a matter of the spirit than a matter of the flesh. We do sin in our flesh, but the real seat of sin is the heart.

Sin seems to have become even more subtle and pervasive in the contemporary age. It continues to be experienced in all its ravaging personal ramifications in man's life. But sin also runs through much of his corporate experience in a modern industrial society. In many respects, the most original thing we can say about man is that he is a sinner.

Notes

1. Unless otherwise noted, historical details in this chapter come from Williston Walker, *A History of the Christian Church* (Edinburgh: T. & T. Clark, 1949).

2. A. F. Kirkpatrick, *The Book of Psalms* (Cambridge: University Press, 1951), p. 290.

3. For further summary of Tertullian's thought in regard to sin, see Reinhold Seebert, *Textbook of the History of Doctrines* (Grand Rapids: Baker Book House, 1956), pp. 122-23.

4. Walker, p. 175.

5. Augustine, *Original Sin,* paragraph 34.

6. For further discussion of Augustine's doctrine of sin, see John H. McClanahan, "The Psychology of the Self in the Writings of Augustine," Unpublished doctoral thesis, The Southern Baptist Theological Seminary, Louisville, KY, May, 1957.

7. For further discussion in this regard, see John Beckwith, *Early Medieval Art* (New York: Thames and Hudson, Inc., 1985), pp. 9-10.

8. Irenaeus, *Heresies* 2:22

9. Walker, pp. 274-75.

10. Roland Bainton, *Here I Stand: A Life of Martin Luther* (New York: Abingdon Press, 1950), p. 72.

11. Ibid., p. 78.

12. Ibid., p. 68.

13. The following information is based primarily on an article by Hugh Watt, "Zwingli," *Encyclopedia of Religion and Ethics* (New York: Charles Scribner's Sons, 1951) 12:873-76.

14. Walker, pp. 392-93.

15. A. B. D. Alexander, "Seven Deadly Sins," *Encyclopedia of Religion and Ethics* (New York: Charles Scribner's Sons, 1951) 11:426-428.

7

What About Sin, Sickness, and Guilt?

The woman talking with me was a patient in the acute care psychiatric unit of a large private hospital in a metropolitan area. I was a chaplain intern, working on the staff of the hospital. Since this patient communicated about her illness in religious terms, her psychiatrist asked me to visit with her for a time on a regular basis.

When I introduced myself as one of the chaplains in the hospital, the woman quickly told me how glad she was to see me. "You see," she said, "I have committed an unpardonable sin. I have done something for which God can never forgive me!"

I told my new friend that I was sorry to learn that she had done something which was causing her such grave concern. Before dealing with that major issue, however, I suggested that we get a bit better acquainted. I asked the lady to tell me something about herself. She seemed happy to do this, and the following story unfolded.

My new friend was happily married and living with her husband and only daughter in a county seat town. The husband's work provided a secure income. This woman was a college graduate, and for a few years before the birth of her daughter, she had taught in the public-school system of her hometown. I guessed she was in her early thirties. She was neatly attractive and expressed herself in clear English. She told me that she and her husband and daughter were active members of a church. She added that earlier in the year, she had been hospitalized for surgery. No malignancy was found in the surgery, and her physical recovery had been satisfactory.

Hearing this informal biographical summary, I did not notice any jagged edges, especially no breach which would point toward the unpardonable sin. So I asked more directly, "How did you come to feel that you have committed the unpardonable sin?"

My friend then told me of a vision which she had experienced a few weeks earlier. The vision occurred on a weekday morning. Her husband had already gone to work, and her young daughter had gone to school. She was alone washing the breakfast dishes at her kitchen sink.

"Suddenly," she said, "I began to hear the most beautiful music. I felt I was being lifted up, out of my kitchen window which was over the sink. I went out and up into the vast blue sky. I went up still higher through the clouds. As I rose higher, the music became stronger and more beautiful. Ahead of me, I saw two great doors—wide open for me to enter. I knew that these doors must be the entrance way to heaven. The beautiful music grew louder, and now there were bright lights. It was a wonderful experience!

"But," she added, "all this was quickly changed. Just before going through the open doors into what must have been the very presence of God, I reached down to take two puffs on my cigarette, which was lying on the edge of the counter near my sink. When I put the cigarette down, the music suddenly stopped and the bright lights were gone. There was a loud slam as the first door to heaven closed, and then another loud slam as the other door closed. I knew that I would never be able to open those doors again. It was all so sad, that I began to cry.

"I had been so close to going right into the presence of God, but that cigarette caused me to lose it all. God is so holy that no one should draw on a cigarette near Him. I was so close, but now it is so far away. That opportunity will never come to me again. Those doors are closed forever. I can't understand why I would do such an awful thing at such a holy moment. I don't think God can ever forgive me for what I did to ruin it all. I feel so guilty."

From a conversation with her doctor, I knew that the surgery the patient had had earlier corrected a gynecological problem. I wanted to understand more about this lady's perception of herself, so I asked her to tell me a little bit about her recent surgery.

Rather openly, she told me that her family doctor at home had recommended that she see a gynecologist for some possible surgery. This new doctor had recommended that she have an ovariotomy. Since she and her husband had very much wanted to have another child, she found it difficult to accept having that kind of surgery. Her surgeon thought one of her ovaries might be saved. However, both ovaries had to be removed.

Although her physical recovery had been good following this surgery, the lady had remained depressed. She was very disappointed that she would not be able to have another child. "My husband was very understanding," she said, "and I did quite well physically. But I don't know whether I will ever get over not being able to be a mother again!"

What was going on in this person's life? On the surface of things, she had become so emotionally depressed in the wake of her surgery that she could not function as a wife and mother. She had rationalized her depression with a religious vision. Her acute depression had caused her to be hospitalized as a psychiatric patient. She was interpreting her depression in terms of having committed an unpardonable sin, for which she felt very guilty. She thought she had done something for which God could never forgive her. Some casual observers might have said that her religious understanding had caused her illness. Her vision could be used as a springboard for a forthright sermon against smoking!

Some irreversible events had occurred in this woman's life. She would never again give birth to a child. Both of her ovaries had been surgically removed. In a real sense, *two* doors had closed in her life experience which were never going to open again. The surgery had brought her a significant loss. This loss pushed her into a bereavement, or grief reaction. She communicated her feelings in religious terms. Her grief was compounded by a sense of guilt which came from her smoking a cigarette when she thought she was so near the doorway to God.

Happily for the person mentioned, adequate psychiatric and pastoral counseling helped her sort out the facts and the feelings in her life situation. In a matter of days, she was able to return to her home. In our last conversation together, she said, "You know I'm not only going home with a better understanding of myself and God, I'm also going home as a person who will be more understanding of other people. I will be a better Christian friend to people in my town because of this stay in the hospital." This actual case history illustrates some of the dimensions of the relationship between sin and sickness and guilt.

Sin and Sickness

What is the relationship between sin and sickness? Do we ever become sick as a direct result of sin in our lives? Is all sickness the result of some kind of sin? Are sin and sickness only imaginary dimensions to life—that is, are they just some fantasy which is "all in our minds"? To what extent are sin and sickness objective realities in our lives? Can a person be sinful without becoming physically ill, that is, can I be sick of soul without being sick in body?

These are not new questions. Such concerns are reflected in the literature of the Bible, as well as in some of the epic stories from other major civilizations. Job, for example, was agonizingly perplexed as to why such great misfortune came upon him, including his being afflicted from head to foot with boils, or "loathsome sores" (2:7).

Job's would-be friends had a very simplistic answer for all of his troubles. They said that Job was suffering because of his sin. Even his boils were the result of wickedness (18:13). Sin equals suffering; therefore, suffering is the result of sin. Why should Job expect to be an exception to this rule?

In fact, the story of Job's life was written down in dramatic form to counter this popular mind-set, which has been known to some extent in every generation. As John D. W. Watts wrote, "It has been thought that there was no such thing as innocent suffering. Job challenges that dogma. Whereas popular doctrine said that piety and prosperity, sin and suffering were absolutely inseparable pairs, Job questions and abolishes the absoluteness of such easy answers to suffering or concomitant problems."[1]

Jesus encountered a similar line of thought in the question that disciples asked Him concerning a certain blind beggar in Jerusalem. Beggars often clustered near the Temple, likely hoping that persons who had so recently worshiped God would be more prone to give to meet human need.

Seeing the beggar, the disciples asked Jesus, "Master, who sinned, this man, or his parents, that he was born blind?" (John 9:2). The disciples took for granted that the beggar's blindness was the result of sin. This was not debatable. The only area open for discussion was *who* had sinned—the beggar himself or his parents?

Jesus, in essence, replied, "Neither!" This man's blindness was not the result of his sin, nor the sin of his parents. To be sure, sometimes sickness can be the result of sin. For example, some blindness is the direct result of eye infections which stem from contact with certain venereal diseases. But not all blindness originates from this cause. Jesus saw the man's physical problem as an opportunity for the grace and power of God to be at work (vv. 3-4). Jesus was much more interested in offering therapy and healing.

To be sure, some illnesses which afflict human beings can be attributed to sin. Excessive personal use of alcohol as a beverage can cause cirrhosis of the liver. Use of tobacco products and exposure to tobacco smoke have been linked to emphysema, lung cancer, and other respiratory ailments. Statistical information from the study of fatalities in auto accidents on the highways has pointed to the fact that "55 Saves Lives!" Drivers who disobey speed limit laws expose themselves and others to a greater possibility of accidental injury and death. Expectant mothers who use illegal drugs during their pregnancies predispose their unborn children to a later dependency upon such drugs in their lives.

As both Job and Jesus declared, however, not all human illness can be attributed to sin and disobedience. There are diseases that, based on present knowledge, have no taint of moral evil. Leukemia appears to be this kind of illness. Communicable diseases like measles, chicken pox, and whooping cough have no direct origin in sin. Certain germs, bacteria, and viruses are loose in the world irrespective of any trail of human sin.

Sin and Sickness Involve the Whole Person

Another straightforward statement can be made relative to sin and sickness: When we experience either of these realities, our total personhood tends to be involved. Sin is not easily restricted to just one area of our lives. Like a raging forest fire, sin may begin as only a small unextinguished match flame, but it quickly spreads to engulf a much larger whole.

As stated in the previous chapter, we never sin in isolation. Other people are always somehow pulled into our predicament of sin. The infection of rampant sin affects the whole of our personal lives—at work, in the family, at the church, in our individual devotional lives, and in our relationships with our friends.

In like manner, any serious illness tends to affect the whole of life. Sensitive physicians are aware that, although their primary area of concern is the specific disease entity which they are treating, they are always treating this illness as it is housed in the total body of a specific human being. How this person thinks and feels about himself will affect to some degree the progress of his recovery. Anxiety, fear, and stress are intangibles as far as a microscope is concerned. These factors can become very real, however, as influences which affect a patient's recovery from a serious illness.

Today psychosomatic medicine is a specific area of medicine that is concerned with the interrelatedness of emotions and body. *Psychosomatic* is a word formed by two Greek roots—*psyche*, which means mind, spirit, or soul, and *soma*, which means body. Although many of us no longer need such a reminder, *psychosomatic* as a single word affirms that the mind and the body are inseparable. When a person is well, it is usually obvious that he is healthy in mind and body. In like manner, when a person is sick, he is likely to be sick in both mind and body.

In her book on this area of medical concern, Dr. Flanders Dunbar wrote, "Illness does not transform a human being into something less. The patient does not become a cardiac or a fracture, an ulcer or a psychopath. He remains as much a person as his healthy brother—more so, if anything. . . . The physician experienced in the psychosomatic approach, therefore, sets out to treat patients as complete human beings."[2]

This holistic approach to understanding and treating the human person is not new. For example, in the more primitive societies of underdeveloped nations, anthropologists have discovered that the ever-present witch doctor fulfilled the roles of what we would call both physician and priest. Soul and body were assumed to be a unity, and one community member cared for both these vital areas.

We should recall that this holistic view of human nature is also a part of the biblical understanding of man. The Greek philosophers had espoused essentially a dualistic view of human personality. Man was a soul in a body. The higher part of man's nature was the soul. The lower part of his nature was the body. The Hebrew-Christian view of human nature, however, is that man is a "body-soul."

D. R. G. Owen wrote succinctly in this regard:

> In short, the Hebrews, though ignorant of the actual physiological nervous system and brain, nevertheless in their own way recognized the dependence of physical activities on the physical organism. The difference is that what modern science centralizes in the brain and nervous system they distributed throughout all the bodily organs. But the Old Testament shares with modern science the same essential idea, namely, the interrelatedness and inseparability of the "body" and the "soul."[3]

Let me share another experience from a pastor's journal which will illustrate the close intertwining of body and soul—what I am calling the psychosomatic understanding of human nature. Several years ago, while being away from my home church in revival services, I received an emergency telephone call from one of the young men in our congregation. He was calling to let me know that his wife had been hospitalized quite unexpectedly. She was facing the possibility of having a part of her right foot amputated. The young husband wanted me to remember him and his wife in my prayers.

I knew this couple quite well. They were active members of the young adult group in our church. Both had just recently graduated from college. The young man had grown up in our church. He and his wife met and married while they were in college. He was now back in his hometown, beginning a promising career in business.

Needless to say, I was shocked to learn that my young friend's wife was facing such a traumatic medical problem. In response to my question, "What on earth has happened?" I learned of this situation.

My friend's wife had what is commonly called a "blood blister" on her right heel. It had been there since birth. Across the years, family doctors had noted the blister and commented that it might someday require some surgical attention. The blue spot, however, had never really given my friend's wife any trouble.

"But yesterday," he was saying, "the blister burst while I was at work and my wife was at home alone. She called me on the phone, and I went home immediately. I found her semihysterical. The place on her foot was hemorrhaging, and blood seemed to be going everywhere in our apartment!"

Wrapping a towel around her foot, my friend rushed his wife to the emergency room of the local hospital. She was seen quickly and transferred to the university medical center in the capital city of our state.

The possibility of amputation had been mentioned by doctors earlier. Now it was a medical recommendation. The young couple was stunned. They had strong support from both their families, but the final decision had to be theirs alone. Due to the radical nature of the proposed surgery, I urged my friend to get at least one second opinion. I assured him of my prayers and told him that I would see him as soon as I got back into town. When I returned home from the revival, I found that young woman's right foot had been amputated. The operation was considered a success, and the patient was going home the next day.

When I visited the couple, I found that the young wife was recovering nicely. In a matter of days, she expected to be walking with crutches. Within two months, she would probably begin wearing some kind of flat walking shoe. During this visit, I sensed that the couple was a bit hesitant to discuss the surgery. They were evidently trying to put the whole ordeal behind them as quickly as possible.

A few Sundays later, the couple was in church for the first time since the surgery. The wife was walking on crutches, and her right leg was still heavily bandaged. They were in church together on two or three other occasions, then at times I would see just the husband in our services. On many Sundays, neither was present. Through a mutual friend, I learned that the couple was visiting some other churches in our city—especially groups which placed much emphasis upon healing services. I sensed this couple was needing some time and space to work through their understanding of the trauma through which they had passed.

After several weeks of seeing very little of this couple, the husband waited to speak to me after a Sunday morning service. He asked if I could come by to see them some time that week. We set a specific time, and I told him I looked forward to seeing both of them.

When I arrived at the couple's home, they were expecting me. We exchanged the pleasantries of the day and then rather quickly the conversation became more serious. The husband mentioned that his wife had something which she wanted to tell me. I sensed that he wanted to be supportive to his wife, yet he was not in full agreement with what she was going to say.

The wife shared with me what she had experienced in a recent revival service in our city. Searching to find additional help in her grave concern about her foot, my friend had been attending a storefront, Pentecostal-type revival meeting. She had gone forward for prayer in one of the closing services of the revival. She said, "All my sins are now forgiven, and I am going to be healed completely. God is going to give me a new foot!"

This young woman was trying to cope with a most difficult intrusion into her early adult life. Her loss must have seemed overwhelmingly great. She was an attractive person, and she must have wondered if she would ever walk normally or be able to wear shoes with real feminine heels.

Trying to be sensitive to the many undercurrents in this situation, I responded to the young wife's story something like this: "You do want me to be honest with you, don't you?"

The husband quickly replied, "That's why we wanted you to come over tonight."

I continued, "Then let me try to say three things to you as honestly and sympathetically as I can." Calling the young wife by her first name, I said, "I too think that you will get a new foot, as a gift from God—when we all get to heaven. In heaven, God has promised that He will 'make all things *new*' (Rev. 21:5). I think that means for you that you will get a new foot. There will be no crutches nor wheel chairs in heaven."

"In the second place," I continued, "I think that you may get a new foot in the here and now when you decide to be fitted with a prosthesis." I went on to describe the great advances which had been made in recent years in the use of artificial limbs. I also said, "My guess is that you would be very surprised to find how well your need in this regard could be met by a specialist trained in this area."

"In the third place," I said, "let me honestly say that I could be wrong. You may wake up some morning and discover that a new foot has grown overnight on your right leg. If that should happen, it would be a miracle from God. If it does happen, I hope you will quickly let me know, and I will praise God with you! . . . But in the meantime, I hope you will check with someone about being fitted with a prosthesis."

I could not tell exactly how my words were received. I had a hunch that the husband heard me somewhat approvingly, but the wife was very skeptical. After all, though, it was her foot, not his, which had been removed. I felt that she was a bit disappointed in me. I was probably a bit less spiritual than she had thought I would be.

A few weeks later, on a Sunday morning as people were entering the sanctuary for the worship hour, I saw this young wife as she came into the church. She was not using crutches. She was dressed in a Sunday outfit and looked quite pretty. She was also wearing neat feminine shoes with a trim heel. Obviously, she had been fitted with a prosthesis, but a casual observer would never have known it!

In a year or so, this couple moved to another city. In time, the wife went to work outside the home. Her job required that she deliver documents to offices in nearby cities. On such an errand one day, she drove her car into an office building lot and parked in a space marked for handicapped persons. She did not happen to see the uniformed guard who was tending this lot.

When she returned to her car, the guard accosted her, "Can't you see?" he said. "You parked in a handicapped space!"

Without saying a word, my attractive young friend opened her car door and sat down on the edge of the driver's seat. Gracefully crossing her legs, she grasped her right foot firmly, twisted it to a right angle, and then stuck it toward the guard.

"Is that handicapped enough for you?" she said.

The guard's eyes almost popped out of his head. "Excuse me, little lady," he blurted, "I had no idea you had a foot like that!"

This actual life situation illustrates quite clearly how we as individuals are psychosomatic wholes. A major physical change in our human bodies can greatly affect how we think and feel about ourselves, about other people, and about God. I thought it noteworthy that the young wife believed for a time that since all her sins were forgiven, God would give her a new foot.

From stunning shock and semihysteria, to partial withdrawal and possible denial, to false hope and religious illusion, to practical acceptance and cunning sense of humor—so my friends had learned to cope with a major psychosomatic problem. Their experience as ordinary Christian people presents a vivid story of how sin, sickness, and guilt can become intertwined in our daily lives.

False Guilt and True Guilt

A sense of guilt played a role in both of the life situations mentioned earlier in this chapter. One person felt that a public confession of sin in a revival service placed her in a better position to receive God's healing. The other person felt that in smoking a cigarette when she was so near the doorway to heaven, she had committed an unpardonable sin.

Neither of these guilt sentiments was well-founded in actual fact. To be sure, the New Testament does report the teaching of Jesus about an unpardonable sin. Jesus defined such a sin as the act of "blasphemy against the [Holy] Spirit" (Matt. 12:31), that is, attributing the work of God and the Holy Spirit to the work of the devil. Jesus did say that "whoever speaks against the Holy Spirit will not be forgiven, either in this age or in the age to come" (v. 32).

While we do have conclusive medical evidence that smoking may be injurious to one's physical health, in no way can we say that two puffs on a cigarette are the equivalent to committing the unpardonable sin. In like manner, as my other friend did learn, an emotional, public confession of sin does not automatically better qualify a person to receive a miraculous gift of healing from God.

Guilt so understood is false guilt. Such a feeling is sometimes called "psychiatric guilt." The sentiment, or feeling, itself can be very genuine. It feels like real guilt, but it is not authentic guilt. The roots of such guilt are often found in confused religious understanding and unresolved physical and psychological concerns. The feeling of guilt is often more the symptom of a problem than the actual problem itself.[4]

All guilt, however, is not symbolic or psychiatric. Bona fide, authentic guilt exists. A psychiatrist said to one of his patients, "Sir, what you have just told me that you have done is wrong. Your behavior goes against both the laws of man and the laws of God. I will be glad to be your friend, but you don't really need to see a doctor. You need to talk to your pastor or your priest!" Wayne Oates spoke of this kind of guilt feeling as the valid "anxiety of sin." He wrote, "Obviously the capacity to sin represents a relatively high state of moral development and *the anxiety of sin is a normal type of anxiety.*"[5]

Guilt and Grace

We come to the close of this study having affirmed anew that man is a sinner. As a sinner, in both his individual and corporate experience, man knows acute, authentic guilt. As the result of his sin, man faces the awesome threat of death and destruction. Man is snared, or trapped, by his sin so that rather than being on a pilgrimage of faith his days on earth become a meaningless treadmill, ultimately ending in death and condemnation.

Wise and well-known lines from the Bible often point to this truth. "None is righteous, no, not one; no one understands, no one seeks for God. All have turned aside, together they have gone wrong; no one does good, not even one" (Rom. 3:10-12; see also Ps. 14:1-2). "All we like sheep have gone astray; we have turned everyone to his own way" (Isa. 53:6a). "All have sinned and fall short of the glory of God" (Rom. 3:23). "The soul that sins shall die" (Ezek. 18:20a). "The wages of sin is death" (Rom. 6:23a). "It is appointed for men to die once, and after that comes judgment" (Heb. 9:27).

From the dark days of World War II and the Nazi blitz bombing of London, England, Leslie Weatherhead told a story of hope which came from one of the British art museums. Great precaution had been taken to protect the art treasures in the London museums, but some galleries were still open to the public during those difficult days.

On one occasion, a museum was displaying an artist's interpretation of Goethe's epic poem, *Faust*. In the painting, Faust and Mephistopheles were seated at a chessboard. Faust, who is symbolic of Everyman in Goethe's poem, was the picture of despair. Mephistopheles, who for Goethe was the incarnation of evil, reflected a state of joy and glee. Looking at the chessboard, it appeared as though Mephistopheles had

Faust cornered. Faust's king was checkmated. The battle between the two opponents was finished. Mephistopheles had won.

One afternoon, an older man, who was a master in the game of chess, was walking with a group of visitors through the gallery. He was fascinated by the scene of the chessboard and the two players. Dropping out of his group, the man sat down in front of the painting to study it in detail. Late that afternoon—just before closing time, the man jumped to his feet and shattered the silence of the gallery, shouting, "It's a lie! It's a lie! The king and the knight can move!"[6] The abject resignation and despair of Faust was ill-founded. The demonic glee of Mephistopheles was not eternal.

This incident is a parable of every person's experience. Man is a sinner. He has been caught by the snare of the evil one. But man's dilemma is not a no win situation. In Jesus Christ, as the King of kings and the Prince of peace, God has moved to bring release and redemption to lost mankind.

Paul expressed this powerfully as he wrote to the Christians in Corinth: "God was in Christ reconciling the world to himself, not counting their trespasses against them. . . . For our sake he made him to be sin who knew no sin, so that in him we might become the righteousness of God" (2 Cor. 5:19*a*, 21).

Notes

1. John D. W. Watts, "Job," *The Broadman Bible Commentary* (Nashville: Broadman Press, 1971) 4:28.

2. Flanders Dunbar, *Mind and Body: Psychosomatic Medicine* (New York: Random House, 1947), p. vii.

3. D. R. G. Owen, *Body and Soul: A Study of the Christian View of Man* (Philadelphia: The Westminster Press, 1956), p. 176.

4. For a more complete and helpful discussion of true guilt and/or false guilt from a psychiatric point of view, see Paul Tournier, *Guilt and Grace* (New York: Harper & Row, 1962), pp. 63-71.

5. Wayne E. Oates, *Anxiety in Christian Experience* (Philadelphia: The Westminster Press, 1955), p. 64.

6. Leslie D. Weatherhead, *Over His Own Signature* (New York: Abingdon Press, 1955), pp. 103-104.

Scripture Index